Yamada-kun and the Seven Witches

1

Miki Yoshikawa

peek

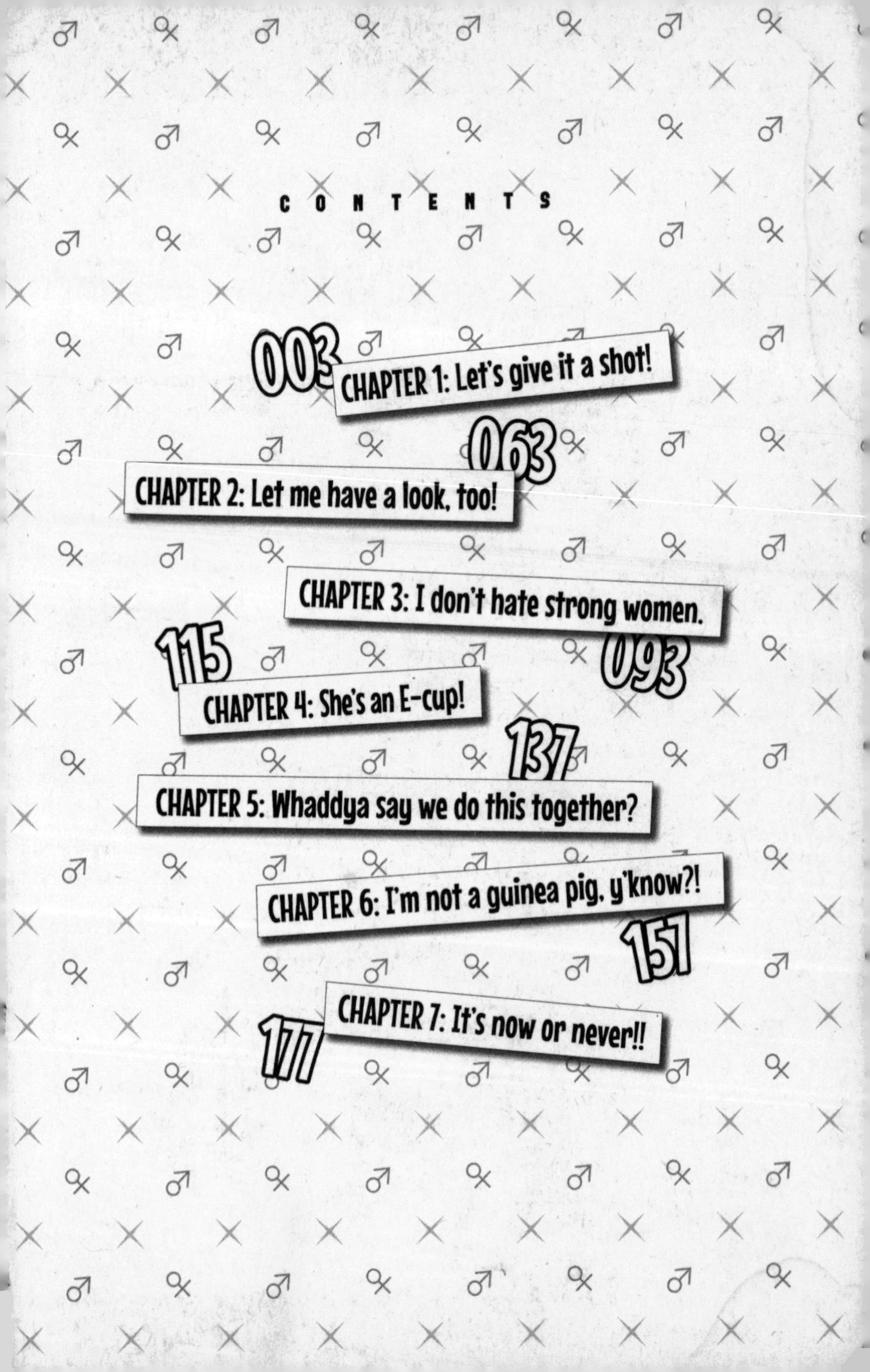

CONTENTS

Once upon a time...
Well, not so long ago, actually,
there was a high school boy known as "Yamada-kun."

Now, Yamada-kun was a so-called "problem child,"
and he was feared by everybody at his school.
But one day,
through a crazy incident,

Yamada-kun
turned into a completely different person...

高等
現代文
Yamada-kun
AND THE
Seven Witches

CHAPTER 1: Let's give it a shot!
高等
現代文

Yamada-kun and the Seven Witches

職員室
STAFFROOM
DO YOU THINK THIS IS SOME KIND OF JOKE?!
EVERY DAY, YOU COME TO SCHOOL LATE AND LEAVE SCHOOL EARLY!
AND NOW YOU'RE SLEEPING IN CLASS?!
THIS IS WHAT YOU GET, RIGHT?!
1st Semester Midterm Results
1学期中間考査結果
Modern Japanese
現代文
15
Classical Literature
古典
8
Math II
数学Ⅱ
20
Math B
数学B
11
English Reading
英語R
6
English
WHAT DO YOU HAVE TO SAY FOR YOURSELF?!
GLOOM
ズーン
MUMBLE
MUMBLE
MUMBLE
SIGH.

TAKE A GOOD LOOK AT YOUR-SELF FOR ONCE!!!
SLAM
TCH!
DAMN IT...
Suzaku Private High School: 2nd Year
RYU YAMADA
I'M FED UP WITH THIS.
STOMP
STOMP
HE LOOKS LIKE BAD NEWS.
THAT'S YAMADA FROM 2ND YEAR. HE'S ONE OF THOSE KIDS WITH ISSUES!
IT'S BEEN A LITTLE OVER A YEAR SINCE I ENTERED HIGH SCHOOL...
AND "FED UP" IS HOW I FEEL ABOUT IT!
I THOUGHT...
HIGH SCHOOL WOULD BE A LITTLE MORE INTER-ESTING!
THEN AGAIN...
I GUESS SCHOOLS THAT PREP YOU FOR COLLEGE ARE LIKE THIS...

STEP
STEP
STEP
STEP
Suzaku Private High School: 2nd Year
URARA SHIRAISHI
HEY, SHE SITS NEXT TO ME...
WHAT WAS HER NAME AGAIN? SHIRAI-SHI?
STEP
STEP
SHE'S ALWAYS HAD THE HIGHEST GRADES IN OUR YEAR...
STEP
AND SHE GOT THE HIGHEST MARK ON OUR MID-TERM!
NO WAY!
EVERY-ONE WAS TALKING ABOUT IT YESTER-DAY...

TCH! AN HONOR STUDENT, HUH?
STOMP
STEP
STOMP
STOMP
STEP
STOMP
STOMP
SNEER
HUH?
SLIP
!

WHA?
THAT'S RIGHT.
THIS WAS WHAT STARTED IT ALL.
EYAAAAAAGHH!!

OHH... DID I...
DID I DIE AND GO TO HEAVEN?
FLUTTER
そよ
FLUTTER
そよ
WHERE AM I?
にぎ
TWITCH
にぎ
TWITCH
ゆさ
WIGGLE
ゆさ
WIGGLE
EXTEND
すっ
?!

SIT-UP
がばっ
HOLD ON!
I'M NOT... DEAD?!!
THIS IS...
THE SCHOOL INFIRMARY, ISN'T IT?!
?
BOING!
...
HUH?!
GROPE
WHAT THE?!
GROPE
GROPE
WHAT IS THIS ?!

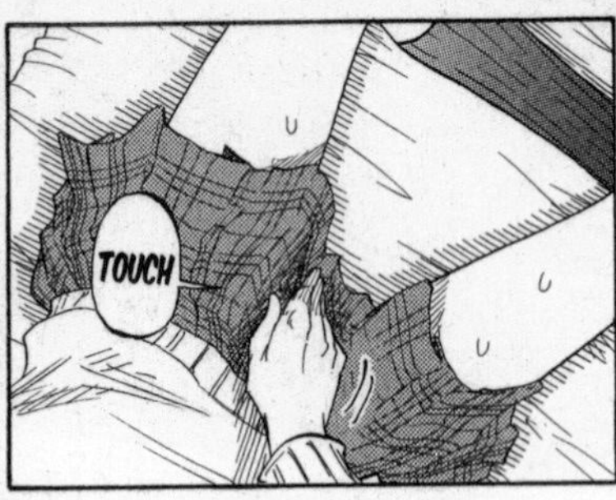
TOUCH

RUB
RUB
RUB

...
THERE'S NOTHING DOWN HERE!!!

シャッ
WHOOSH!

OH!
YOU'VE WOKEN UP!
MIRROR!
W-WHAT THE HELL IS GOING ON?
?
パタパタ
FOOTSTEPS
TUG
TUG
I...
SQUEEZE

I'M HER?!

STAND
すたっ
YOU GAVE EVERYONE QUITE A SCARE!
BOTH YOU AND YAMADA-KUN FELL DOWN THE STAIRS...
WHOOSH
シャッ
LUCKILY, YOU ONLY SUFFERED A SMALL CONCUSSION.
SHE'S NOT HERE!

IF YOU'RE LOOKING FOR YAMADA-KUN, HE ALREADY WOKE UP AND WENT TO CLASS!
OHH ...
WHAT ?!
RATTLE
HEY, HOLD ON!
YOU SHOULD STILL GO TO THE HOSPITAL!
STEP
STEP
HOLD ON A SEC!
STOMP
STOMP
STOMP
STOMP
WHO RUNS LIKE THAT?!
STOMP
SO SHE'S INSIDE MY BODY, THEN, IS THAT IT?!
SHE'S GOING TO CLASS LIKE THAT?
PANT!
PANT!
RATTLE
2-A
WHAT THE HELL IS SHE THINKING?!

ACK!
どーん
SCRIB
SCRIB
SCRIB
SCRIB
SCRIB
SCRIB
SCRIB
?!!
W-WHAT'S UP WITH THAT YAMADA GUY?!
MURMUR ざわ
HE'S SITTING WITH HIS KNEES TOGETHER...
MURMUR ざわ
MURMUR ざわ
WAS THAT GUY ALWAYS SUCH A BOOKWORM?!

RATTLE がたっ
SIR?
IN THIS CASE, ARE ANSWERS A AND C INTER-CHANGE-ABLE?

UH...
THEY ARE, BUT...

WHAT THE—

BAM
WHAT THE HELL ARE YOU DOING?!
YANK!
LET'S GO, BUDDY!
CLATTER
CLATTER
THUD
WHY?
BUT WE'RE IN CLASS...
DAMN IT, CAN'T YOU TELL BY LOOKING AROUND?! ARE YOU CRAZY?
WHO GIVES A DAMN ABOUT CLASS?!
THUD
CLATTER
LET'S GO ALREADY!!
DRAG DRAG
SLAM
...

WHAT THE HELL IS GOING ON?!
HOW DID YOU AND I...
...SWITCH BODIES?!
...
I DON'T KNOW.
Y-YOU DON'T KNOW?!
HOW CAN YOU STAY SO CALM RIGHT NOW?!
YOU'RE GOING TO CLASS LIKE IT'S NO BIG DEAL!
DO YOU KNOW WHAT THIS MEANS FOR THE BOTH OF US?!
Math II
数学II

FOR THE MOST PART.
THEN WHY-
WHY THIS HAPPENED TO US,
I DON'T KNOW.
BUT...

I THINK I KNOW HOW TO GET US BACK...
...TO THE WAY WE WERE.
Math II
数学II

WHAT?!

WELL IF YOU THINK ABOUT IT,
IT ALL STARTED WITH US FALLING DOWN THE STAIRS...
SO IF WE DO THE SAME THING AGAIN, WE'LL PROBABLY GO BACK TO NORMAL!

WHOEVER CAN'T FIGURE *THAT* OUT IS PRETTY SAD.
YOU'VE GOT A PRETTY CRAPPY ATTITUDE, YA KNOW THAT?!
Math II
数学II

OKAY, WHAT-EVER!
LET'S HURRY UP AND HEAD FOR THE STAIRS THEN!
I DON'T THINK SO.
Math
数学
HUH?!
WELL, THAT MEANS WE'LL HAVE TO FAINT AGAIN, RIGHT?
SHUT
AND I CAN'T MISS ANY MORE CLASSES THAN I ALREADY HAVE!
WHAT?!
IS THIS GIRL FOR REAL?!

T-THEN, WHAT ARE YOU SAYING?
YOU WANNA STAY LIKE THIS FOREVER?!
NO, I DON'T WANT THAT EITHER.
I DON'T LIKE HAVING SOMETHING STRANGE BETWEEN MY LEGS.
Y-YOU LOOKED DOWN THERE?!

JUST WAIT UNTIL AFTER SCHOOL.
AFTER SCHOOL ?!
IT SHOULD BE FINE. NO ONE WILL EVER REALIZE WHAT HAP-PENED...
IF YOU DON'T DRAW ATTENTION TO YOUR-SELF, THAT IS!
YOU DRAW MORE THAN ENOUGH ATTENTION FOR THE BOTH OF US!
IN ANY CASE...
KERCHAK!
ガチャッ
YOU'LL JUST HAVE TO ACCEPT MY TERMS.
BESIDES, WE ENDED UP THIS WAY...
SLAM
...BECAUSE YOU TRIPPED AND FELL DOWN THE STAIRS.
JOLT
ギクリッ
...NGH!
WELL... TECHNICALLY, THAT'S TRUE BUT...

THIS ISN'T RIGHT!!
STOMP
STOMP
WHAT THE HELL AM I SUPPOSED TO DO IN THIS BODY?!
PAUSE
WAIT! WHAT AM I SAYING?!
THIS IS MY ONE CHANCE!
Ladies' Restroom
女子トイレ
SLAM
VOOM
VA-

RUMBLE
RUMBLE
RUMBLE
WOWOW
WOWOW
WOW!!!
?
PEEK
DANG
DONG
DING
DONG
SIGH.
MAN, WHY DO I FEEL SO GUILTY ...?
I MEAN, I JUST SAW SOME-THING AMAZING!
BAH! WHO CARES?! SHE SAW MY PARTS, TOO!
HEY, YOU! CAN YOU TAKE THESE TO THE MATH DEPARTMENT FOR ME?

YOU WANT ME TO WHAT?!
?
UH... I MEAN, CERTAINLY! I'LL GET RIGHT ON IT!
THAT WAS CLOSE!

DAMN IT!
2-B
のっし
UMPH
のっし
UMPH
WHY DO I GOTTA DO CRAP LIKE THIS?

OH!
NOTE
ばっしゃあっ
CRASH
AW, YOU GOTTA BE KIDDING ME!!
HEY, ARE YOU ALL RIGHT?

LET ME HELP YOU!!
PANT
PANT
UH, NO! LEMME!
PANT
PANT
NO!! ALLOW ME!!

UGH...
PANT
PANT
PANT
THIS CREEPS ME OUT!

BUT I GOTTA PUT ON THE ACT!
IT'S OKAY! TEE HEE! ♥

TCH!
WHAT'S UP WITH SHIRAISHI-SAN TODAY?
SHE USUALLY GIVES US THE DEATH STARE...
NEVER MIND THAT. WHY IS SHE WALKING LIKE THAT, SHOWING OFF HER PANTIES?
Math Department
数学科
I BROUGHT THE NOTE-BOOKS...
OH, THANKS! DO YOU MIND PUTTING THEM OVER HERE?

RIIIGHT OVER HERE...
...
STARE
JUST HOLD IT IIIN!
Campos
MATH II

GOSH, SIR!
PLEASE STOP THAT! ♥
SLAM
ピシャッ
HUH?
HOW COME SHE DIDN'T GLARE AT ME AND SAY THAT'S "SEXUAL HARASSMENT"?!
IT MAKES ME FEEL LIKE I'M ACTUALLY SEXUALLY HARASSING HER!
BUT YOU ARE.
GROAAAN...
ずーーーん...
SIGH... MAN, THIS GIRL...
SHE SURE HAS IT ROUGH EVERY DAY.

I'M SICK OF IT ALREADY
I WISH I COULD HURRY UP AND SWITCH BODIES!
WELL, WELL! LOOK WHO I FOUND!

LET'S HAVE LUNCH TOGETHER!
2nd Year, Class B
RIN SASAKI

?
GEEZ, WHAT WERE YOU DOING?
WE WERE LOOKING ALL OVER FOR YOU!
THESE GIRLS ARE IN OUR CLASS...
BUT SHIRAISHI'S A TOP STUDENT ...
DOES SHE REALLY HANG OUT WITH THESE IDIOTS?
LET'S EAT IN THE COURTYARD TODAY!
UM... OKAY.
LET'S JUST PLAY ALONG FOR NOW.

LET'S EAT!
AREN'T YOU GONNA EAT?
OH... YEAH.
IT'S HER LUNCH...BUT I GUESS IT'S OKAY TO EAT IT.
POP!
ぐっちゃあ…
MESSY...
UH...

...
WHA-
WHAT THE HELL?
THIS IS THE LUNCH OF AN HONOR STUDENT?!

WELL, I HAVE NO IDEA WHAT ALL THIS IS ABOUT,
BUT IT SURE DOES TASTE GOOD!
GOBBLE GOBBLE
ガツガツ
PFT FT FT
ププププ
HEH! HEH! HEH!
クスクスクス
?
OH! I ALMOST ORGOT!
WE HAVE A QUIZ IN OUR NEXT CLASSICAL LIT CLASS!
MAYBE WE SHOULD PREP FOR IT NOW!
DID YOU BRING YOUR TEXT-BOOK?
YEAH, I HAVE IT RIGHT HERE.
FLIP...
パラ...
!
Classical Literature II
古典二

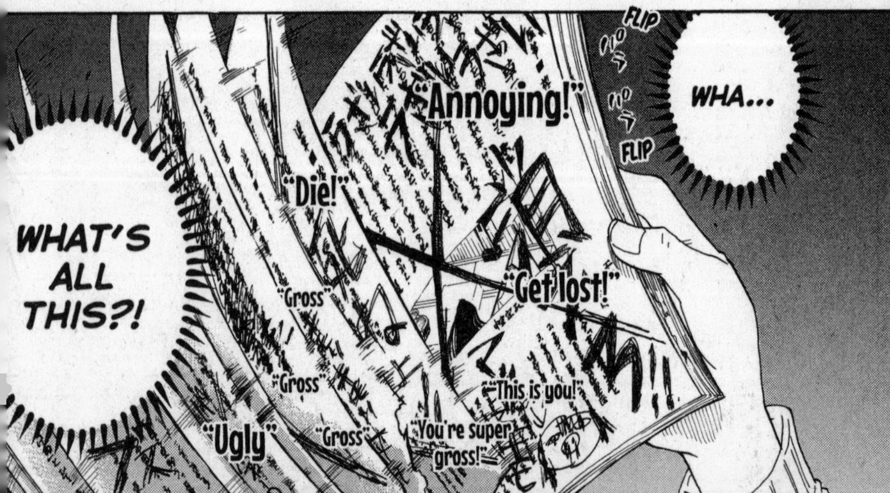

FLIP
パラ
パラ
FLIP
WHA...
"Annoying!"
"Die!"
"Get lost!"
"Gross"
"Gross"
"This is you!"
"Ugly"
"Gross"
"You're super gross!"
WHAT'S ALL THIS?!

THESE AREN'T HER NOTES, ARE THEY?!
THIS IS NO JOKE!
BFFFT
ブフーッ
?
OKAY, GIRLS!
WE SHOULD GET READY TO GO TO OUR NEXT CLASS!

KA-CHAK
カチャッ
!
TUMBLE
TUMBLE
TUMBLE
PFT!
HEH HEH!

AHAHA-HAHA!
GLARE
I SEE HOW IT IS...
WHAT? YOU GOT A PROBLEM?!
"Idiot"
ばか
"Annoying"
"Idiot"
"Die!"
"Die!"
"Die!"
"Die!"
"You're disgusting. Why don't you go kill yourself?"
"Don't come to school!"
"Get lost!"
"Die!"
"Die!"
"Get lost!"
SO THIS IS WHAT'S REALLY GOING ON...

MAN, GIRLS SURE DO PLAY DIRTY!
IT AIN'T EASY BEING A GIRL!

...
EVERY-THING THEY DO IS DIRTY!
I CAN'T BELIEVE ALL THAT GOES ON BEHIND THE SCENES!
AND YOU!
WHY DIDN'T YOU SAY ANYTHING ABOUT THIS, HUH?!

THANKS TO YOU, I GOT SCREWED WITH BIG TIME!
...
TURN
HEY! YOU IGNORING ME?!

I'M SORRY.
I NEVER THOUGHT YOU WOULD GET TANGLED UP WITH SASAKI-SAN AT LUNCH TIME.
SHALL WE GO, THEN?
IT'S PROBABLY BETTER THAT WE SWITCH BODIES NOW.
NO WAY!
OH?
YOU DON'T WANT TO MISS ANY MORE CLASS, DO YOU?
I REAL-IZED SOME-THING BEING IN THIS BODY!
I ALWAYS THOUGHT OF YOU AS A STUCK-UP HONOR STUDENT,
BUT YOU ACTUALLY HAVE IT PRETTY ROUGH.
WE'RE GONNA DO IT AFTER SCHOOL LIKE WE AGREED!

SO I DECIDED I'M GONNA BE ON YOUR SIDE WITH THIS ONE!
BY THE TIME WE SWITCH BACK TO NORMAL,
I'LL MAKE SURE THOSE MORONS NEVER BOTHER YOU AGAIN!
AND BESIDES, ON A PERSONAL NOTE...
THOSE GIRLS REALLY GOT ON MY NERVES!

SOUND GOOD?
GRIP
ガッ
ACK! WHAT THE-

DON'T SCREW AROUND WITH ME!!
OLT
びくっ
HUH?
I DON'T NEED SOME GUY MEDDLING IN MY BUSINESS, ALL RIGHT?
IT'LL ONLY MAKE THINGS WORSE!!
WHY DO YOU THINK I'VE BEEN PUTTING UP WITH IT UNTIL NOW?!
...
ARE WE CLEAR?!
THIS IS A "GIRL THING," OKAY?!
NO BOYS STICKING THEIR NOSE WHERE IT DOESN'T BELONG!

...
GLANCE

OH YEAH?!

SO WHAT EXACTLY HAPPENED OVER THERE?

OVER WHERE ?
DON'T PLAY DUMB!

WHAT WERE YOU AND YAMADA TALKING ABOUT ON THE ROOF-TOP?!

NOT MUCH.
IT'S NOTHING YOU NEED TO WORRY ABOU—

WHACK
?!
DON'T PLAY WITH ME!
TSK!

YOU NO-GOOD TRAMP! CLINGING ONTO SOME GUY LIKE THAT!
AND TO HAVE YAMADA STAND BY YOU, OF ALL PEOPLE!

OHH...WHEN SHE SAW SHIRAISHI COMING TO TALK TO ME...
SHE GOT IT IN HER HEAD THAT WE WERE SCHEMING TOGETHER!
MAN, GIRLS ARE SUCH A PAIN!
WHAT CAN YAMADA DO FOR YOU, ANY-WAY?

THAT PIECE OF SCHOOL TRASH!
HE'S A NO-GOOD, STUPID LONER!
HE'S SCUM!
TWITCH
OH?

SO IS HE GOING TO SPREAD A RUMOR ABOUT ME IN SCHOOL?
OR WHAT? IS HE GONNA TELL THE TEACHERS?

EVEN IF HE DOES, NO ONE WOULD EVER BELIEVE HIM!
OR IS HE GONNA LAY A HAND ON A LI'L GIRL LIKE ME?
NO MATTER HOW DUMB HE IS, EVEN HE KNOWS WHAT WOULD HAPPEN TO HIM IF HE DID THAT!
STEP
YEAH ...

YOU'RE RIGHT!
WHA ...
WHAT DO YOU MEAN?!
I'VE BEEN GETTING A LITTLE BORED, SEE?
STEP
ざっ
STEP
ざっ
THERE ISN'T ANYONE AT THIS SCHOOL THAT I CAN CALL A "RIVAL"!

STEP
STEP
WHA... WHAT IS THIS ALL OF A SUDDEN?!
YOU'RE N-NOT GONNA FIGHT BACK NOW, ARE YOU?
I-IT'S NOT GONNA SOLVE ANYTHING, YOU KNOW?!
Y-YOU DON'T REALLY THINK YOU CAN GET AWAY WITH IT, DO YOU?!
WHY DO YOU THINK I'VE BEEN PUTTING UP WITH IT UNTIL NOW?!
THAT'S WHY THEY WALK ALL OVER THE HONOR STUDENT!
GRIP
IF I GIVE HER THE SCARE OF HER LIFE JUST ONCE,
SHE'LL LEARN TO BEHAVE REAL QUICK!!

BAM

WHA ...
ZM
ZM
ZM
WHAT DO YOU THINK YOU'RE DOING?
ZM
NO...
ZM
WATCH OU-
KA-POW

YOU–
YOU IDIOT!!
KRRRASH
YOU MADE ME HIT YOU, DAMN IT!!!
SSSH
I WASN'T PLANNING ON ACTUALLY HITTING HER, YOU KNOW?!
YOU JUST HAD TO GET IN THE WAY, DIDN'T YOU?!
WHA...
WHAT WAS THAT?!

HEY, YOU!
SIT-UP
!
THROB
OWW!
YOU REALLY HIT ME HARD!

SHOCK
HUHH ?!!
TREMBLE
OH, SHADDUP! THAT'S WHAT YOU GET!
TREMBLE

WHY DID YOU GET INVOLVED?
AFTER EVERYTHING I TOLD YOU!!
SHRIEK
ギャー
SHRIEK
ギャー
SHUT UP!
IT'S 'CAUSE YOU WON'T DO ANYTHING ABOUT IT!
SHOUT
わー
SHOUT
わー
UU...
UU...

ZOOM
ぴゅ
EYAAA AAAA AGH!!!
!

...
HUH?

キーンコーン
DING DONG
カーンコーン…
DANG DONG

OH... CLASS IS ABOUT TO START!
たっ
TURN
ええーー!!?
WHAAAT?!!
YOU'RE REALLY GONNA GO TO CLASS AFTER ALL THAT?!!

GEEZ.
WHAT A PAIN!

After School
DA-DUM
FINALLY, WE CAN SWITCH BACK TO NORMAL!
BECAUSE THIS HAD TO HAPPEN WITH YOU OF ALL PEOPLE, MY IMAGE IS ON THE LINE NOW.
THIS DAY HAS BEEN JUST THE WORST!
YOU TOOK THE WORDS RIGHT OUT OF MY MOUTH.

S-STILL, WILL YOU BE OKAY?
WHAT ABOUT THAT SASAKI GIRL?
ISN'T SHE GOING TO BOTHER YOU AGAIN?
I DON'T KNOW.
JOLT
BUT ...
WHEN I SAW SASAKI TURN TAIL AND RUN LIKE THAT...

I THOUGHT, "TAKE THAT!"
SO THANKS.
UH!
OH...
SURE!
SHE'S A LOT SWEETER THAN I THOUGHT.

WELL THEN, SHALL WE?
RIGHT.
AND SO, THAT'S HOW THE TWO OF US...

SSSSH
OUCH...
...WERE ABLE TO TURN BACK TO NORMAL.
!
!

...
OR SO WE THOUGHT...!

えええええええ!!?
WHAAAAAAAAA?!!
IT...
IT DIDN'T WORK!!!
WHAT WENT WRONG?!
YOU FELL THE WRONG WAY, DIDN'T YOU?!
EXCUSE ME?! YOU PROBABLY GOT DISTRACTED!
WHATEVER WE'RE DOING IT ONE MOR TIME!
IF WE WERE ABLE TO SWITCH BODIES BEFORE...
...THEN THERE'S GOTTA BE A WAY TO SWITCH BACK, TOO!

ズーン
GLOOM
IT'S NO USE.

WHY?!
WHY ISN'T IT WORKING?!
ARE WE...
...STUCK IN THESE BODIES... FOREVER?!!

DAMN IT!!
...
WHAT THE HELL ARE WE GONNA DO?!
OPEN YOUR MOUTH AND SAY SOME-THING!!
?
...WHAT IS IT?
!
THERE'S STILL...
...ONE THING WE HAVEN'T TRIED YET.
GRAB
W-WHAT IS IT?
SPIT IT OUT!!
WHEN WE FELL DOWN THE STAIRS...

WE KISSED.
SHOVE
HUHH HHHH HH?!!
WH- WHAT?!
ARE YOU LOSING IT?!
DON'T ASK ME!
YOU FELL ON TOP OF ME.
...

LET'S GIVE IT A SHOT.
UH!
C'MON! SITTING AROUND DOING NOTHING ISN'T GONNA SOLVE ANYTHING, IS IT?!
BU...
WAI...
I...
ARE WE...
REALLY...
...

HEY... I'M BACK!
SEE?
SMILE
にこっ
DIDN'T I TELL YOU?
...
WELL, I SHOULD GO HOME! I HAVE STUDIES TO DO!
TURN
たっ
HUH?! HEY!
...
DAMN.
THAT GIRL...

SHE GOT ME GOOD...!!
AND SO, JUST LIKE THAT...
...WE WERE BACK TO OUR NORMAL SELVES.

BUT THE NEXT DAY...
THINGS TOOK AN UNEXPECTED TURN AT SCHOOL!
YESTERDAY, SHIRAISHI-SAN TOTALLY FLIPPED,
AND APPARENTLY SHE BEAT THE CRAP OUT OF THAT YAMADA KID!
SHE MUST BE SCARY AS HELL TO MAKE A THUG LIKE HIM SUBMIT TO HER!

SHUDDER
WHOA! EVERYONE'S AFRAID OF HER NOW!

IT'S FINE. NOW NO ONE COMES NEAR ME
SO I CAN FINALLY FOCUS ON MY STUDIES.
ENGLISH
SHIRAISHI HERSELF DIDN'T SEEM TO MIND ALL THAT MUCH.
BUT AS FOR ME...
STARE
I COULDN'T SHAKE THE FEELING THAT SASAKI-SAN WAS ALWAYS WATCHING ME...
BUT I'LL WORRY ABOUT THAT LATER.
GA-THAK
YO, SHIRAISHI!
ABOUT YESTERDAY ...
YOU DIDN'T HESITATE TO *KISS* ME, HUH?
WHAT?
SO...
THAT MEANS...

YOU ACT LIKE AN HONOR STUDENT...
BUT YOU'RE REALLY A NAUGHTY LITTLE VIXEN!
ニヤッ
GRIN
ニヤ
GRIN
ニヤ
GRIN
ニヤ
GRIN

GOD, YOU'RE DUMB.
WHAT?!!
Suzaku High School
朱雀高等学校

Yamada-kun and the Seven Witches

Student Council Meeting Room
生徒会室
RYU YAMADA, THE ONE IN SECOND YEAR, CLASS B?

YES, PRESIDENT. SINCE LAST YEAR, HE'S FREQUENTLY COME UP AS A PROBLEM IN OUR MEETINGS!
WE'VE LOST COUNT AS TO HOW MANY TIMES HE'S CAUSED TROUBLE SINCE COMING TO THIS SCHOOL!

HE GETS LO
GRADES, HE'S DIS
RUPTIVE I
CLASS...
...AND HE REPEATEDLY COMES TO SCHOOL LATE AND LEAVES EARLY!
NOT ONLY THAT, HE GETS INTO FIGHTS WITH STUDENTS FROM OTHER SCHOOLS EVERY DAY!

THERE HAVE BEEN SEVERAL COMPLAINTS DIRECTED AT THE STUDENT COUNCIL ABOUT THIS.

...I SEE.

SUZAKU HIGH SCHOOL IS KNOWN AS ONE OF THE MOST PRESTIGIOUS ACADEMIC INSTITUTIONS...
NOD
IT'S HARD TO BELIEVE A STUDENT LIKE THAT ATTENDS OUR SCHOOL.
SO... WHAT SHOULD BE DONE ABOUT THIS "YAMADA" FELLOW?
RIGHT, PRESIDENT.

TODAY, THERE IS A CHANCE...
...THAT YAMADA-KUN WILL BE EXPELLED!

CHAPTER 2: Let me have a look, too!

READY?
OKAY.
THA-THUMP ドキ
THUMP ドキ
THA-THUMP ドキ
!

TA-DAH
WHAT?!
W-WE SWITCHED BODIES... AGAIN?!
WELL, IT LOOKS LIKE OUR EXPERIMENT PROVES IT!
PEEK
THE TIME AND PLACE DOESN'T REALLY MATTER, AFTER ALL!
WHITE AGAIN, HUH?
WHICH MEANS, WE CAN SWITCH BODIES...
...JUST BY KISSING!

WH-WHAT?! IS THIS FOR REAL?!
THIS IS SOME CRAZY STUFF, MAN!
YOU'VE ONLY JUST NOTICED THAT...
I DON'T KNOW HOW THIS IS POSSIBLE, BUT...
ONE THING'S FOR SURE...

THIS IS AN INCREDIBLE POWER...!

TUG
HEY!
AND THEN ...
NO WAY!
...

WHY ARE WE HIDING?
ISN'T IT OBVIOUS?
I CAN'T HAVE ANY MORE WEIRD RUMORS GOING AROUND ABOUT US!
THINGS GOT MESSY ENOUGH AFTER THAT LAST INCIDENT!

...YOU HAVE A POINT THERE.
WE SHOULD PROBABLY SWITCH BACK, THEN.
YEAH, THAT WOULD BE GOOD!

THEN...
はしっ
I HAVE ONE SUGGESTION TO MAKE...
くいっ
PULL
LET'S KEEP THIS A SECRET BETWEEN YOU AND ME.

はっ
FWIP
!
WHAT DO YOU SAY?

O-OBVI-OUSLY!!
YOU THINK I COULD TELL PEOPLE ABOUT THIS?!
SMILE
にこっ
GOOD.

...
WELL, I HAVE TO STUDY, SO I'M GONNA GO!

SHE SURE IS HAPPY ABOUT KEEPING IT A "SECRET."

HMM...
SO, I CAN BECOME SHIRAISHI ANY TIME NOW, HUH?
SHUFFLE
ずっか
SHUFFLE
ずっか
STILL, AFTER THE MESS THAT HAPPENED THE LAST TIME I TURNED INTO A GIRL, I THINK I'LL PASS!
...AND ON TOP OF THAT,
I HAVE TO KISS SHIRAISHI EVERY SINGLE TIME, TOO!
I WONDER WHY IT'S SO EASY FOR HER TO JUST KISS ME...?!
SCRATCH SCRATCH
ポリ ポリ
LIKE WITH THAT EXPERIMENT WE JUST DID...
PAUSE
COULD IT BE...?!

IT'S BECAUSE I LIKE YOU, YAMADA-KUN!
N...
NO WAY!
UG

!

NOTICE
The following students must take their make-up test for the mid-term examination.
2nd Year, Class B
RYU YAMADA
WAIT... THAT WAS... TODAY?!

Furthermore, a score below 80% will result in **expulsion** from this school.
STOMP STOMP STOMP
ドタタタタ
I TOTALLY FORGOT!!!
CRAP...
...SO THAT'S WHY...
CLAP
...I'M BEGGING YOU!!!
...
I MEAN, I KNOW YOU'RE BUSY WITH STUDYING AND ALL, BUT...
...I'M IN SERIOUS TROUBLE HERE!!
英単語 4000
Super Tough English Vocab 4000

I'M BEGGING YOU!!
SWITCH BODIES WITH ME AND TAKE THE MAKE-UP TEST, PLEASE!!

SHUT
?
Super Tough English Vocab 4000
PEEK

SURE, NO PROBLEM.

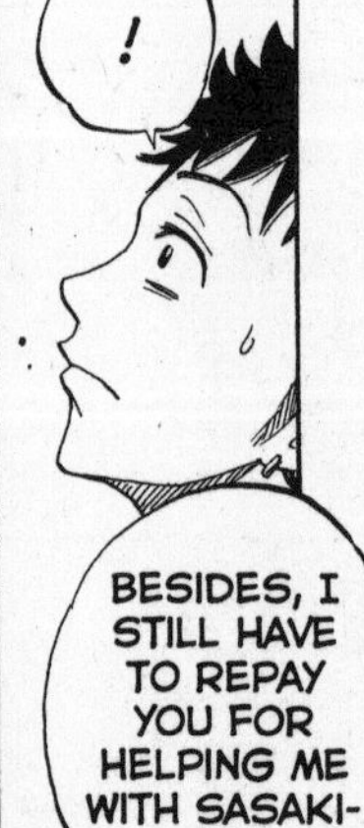
!
BESIDES, I STILL HAVE TO REPAY YOU FOR HELPING ME WITH SASAKI-SAN.

A-ARE YOU SURE?!
YOU KNOW THIS MEANS YOU WON'T BE ABLE TO STUDY, RIGHT?
WHAT ARE YOU TALKING ABOUT? THE MAKE-UP TEST *IS* STUDYING.
NO WONDER YOU HAVE THE BEST GRADES IN OUR YEAR...

Meeting Room
会議室
WITH THAT, WE WILL NOW HOLD THE MAKE-UP TEST...
YOU MAY BEGIN!
ピラッ
FLIP

"Join the Basketball Club!!"
部員募集!!
バスケットボール部
Make-up Exam
追試
PHEW!

WHO'DA THOUGHT I'L GET OUT OF A JAM LIKE THIS?!
SHE SURE CAN COME IN HANDY!

おーーい!
HEY!
URARA-CHAN, CLASS IS ABOUT TO START!

くるっ
TURN
BE RIGHT THERE!
I GUESS I GOTTA ACT LIKE SHIRAISHI AND HEAD TO CLASS!

GULP!

TEE HEE
キャイ♥
P.E. ...OF ALL CLASSES!!!
TEE HEE
キャイ♥
TEE HEE
キャイ♥
キャイ♥
TEE HEE

LOOKS LIKE WE'RE PLAYING HANDBALL IN THE SCHOOLYARD TODAY!
CHATTER
わい
NOT AGAIN!
CHATTER
わい
CHATTER
わい
IT'S TOO COLD TO WEAR SHORTS!
I KNOW!
わい
CHATTER
H-HOLY SMOKES! FRONT ROW SEATS TO THE GIRLS' CHANGING ROOM!
AND IT SMELLS GOOD TOO!

SLIP
HUH?!
SLIP
WH-WHA?!
LET'S GO, GIRLS!
CROWD
ぞろ
CROWD
ぞろ
朝ごはんを食べよう!!
WHAAAT?!
えええええーー!!?
THEY WERE SO FAST I COULDN'T SEE A THING!!
MAN, THAT WAS LAME!
ぬぎ
UNDRES
UNDRESS
ぬぎ
THAT WAS NOTHING LIKE THE GIRLS' LOCKER ROOM I IMAGINED!
FWUF
ふぁさっ
NOT SO FAST, URARA-CHAN!

!
YOU GOTTA BE A BIT MORE CAREFUL WHEN YOU CHANGE YOUR CLOTHES!
?
DON'T YOU KNOW WHAT'S BEEN GOING ON LATELY?
"GOING ON"?
THERE'S A *PEEP PHOTOGRAPHER!*
WHAT?!
SCARY, EH? SOME GIRLS EVEN SAID THEY'VE SEEN SOMEONE AT THE WINDOW!
YUP!
AND THE LOCKER ROOM WAS EVEN FOUND OPEN, WITH THE CURTAINS PULLED BACK!

SOME GIRLS ARE SO SCARED THAT THEY'V STARTED CHANGING I THE BATH-ROOM!
AND WHEN WE TELL THE TEACHERS, THEY DON'T DO MUCH MORE THAN TELL US TO "EXERCISE CAUTION"!
URARA-CHAN, SINCE YOU'RE POPULAR WITH THE BOYS, YOU'D BETTER BE CAREFUL!
!

HMMM...
ほーう!
MAN, SHIRAISHI SURE IS UNEX-PECTEDLY POPULAR...
WHATEVER, IT'S NOT LIKE I HAVE ANYTHING TO DO WITH THIS!
YOU KNOW WHAT?

I BET *YAMADA* IS BEHIND ALL THIS!
WHAT THE?!

I MEAN, HE'S ALWAYS SKIPPING P.E. CLASS, RIGHT?
NOW THAT YOU MENTION IT!
YOU'RE RIGHT! IT MUST BE HIM!
DON'T BE STUPID!! WHY THE HELL WOULD I DO THAT?!
WHAT?
OH... UH, I MEAN...
YAMADA-KUN...
WOULD NEVER DO SOMETHING LIKE THAT! ♥
YOU NEVER KNOW!
WHAT?!
HE'S PRETTY FAMOUS FOR BEING A TROUBLE-MAKER!
I MEAN, HE EVEN LOOKS LIKE TROUBLE!
BESIDES, I'VE HEARD THAT SOME PEOPLE HAVE ACTUALLY SEEN HIM SNAPPING PICS AND RUNNING AWAY!
NO WAY!

DAMN IT. WHY THE HELL...
...DO THEY THINK IT'S ME?!!
RUSTLE RUSTLE
ガサ
ガサ
!

?
C'MON, LET'S GO!
朝ごはんを食べよう!

RUSTLE
ガサ
RUSTLE
ガサ
ガサッ
RUSTLE
WHAT'S THAT NOISE?

ガラッ
SLIDE

SNAP
RUSTLE
RUSTLE
RUSTLE
RUSTLE

NOW YOU'RE ASKING FOR IT!!

...SO, HOW'D IT GO?

HERE YA GO!
FEAST YOUR EYES ON THIS!

OH YEAH, BABY!
WE'VE GOT A HOT ONE HERE!
I KNOW, MAN! WHAT LUCK HAVIN' URARA SHIRAISHI POKE HER HEAD OUT!
THIS ONE'S GONNA GO FOR A HIGH PRICE!
HEY! LEMME HAVE A LOOK, TOO!
BUT, I WONDER IF IT'S OKAY THAT SHE'S STARIN' STRAIGHT AT US IN THIS PICTURE.
IT'S COOL, MAN! GIRLS ARE TOO SCARED TO DO ANYTHIN' 'BOUT IT, ANYWAY!
I SAID, LET ME HAVE A LOOK!

HUH?!
SHOW. ME.
GRIN

WHAAAAAAA!
うわあああ
WHA—
WHAT THE HELL IS URARA SHIRAISHI DOIN' HERE?!
SHUT UP!
SO YOU GUYS WERE THE SICKOS WHO WERE PEEPING!
H-HEY, JUST H-HOLD ON, OKAY?!
Y-YA GOT IT ALL WRONG!
N-NOW THAT YOU MENTION IT...
I DID SEE YAMADA RUNNIN' AWAY IN A PANIC A WHILE AGO!
THROB
THERE'S NO CHANCE IN HELL THAT'S TRUE!
THROB
THROB
ゴゴゴゴ
RUMBLE RUMBLE RUMBLE RUMBL
I KNOW WHERE YAMADA IS...
SHE KNOWS?!
JOLT
ビクッ
ぎゃあああ
HE'S TAKING MY MAKE-UP TEST!!
AAAGHHH!!!
あああ

TA-DAH
どーん!!
...
UM... SO...
YOU CAUGHT THEM?
STOMP
ドッカ
STOMP
ドッカ
STOMP
ドッカ
TCH!

OH, SHOOT!
THE MAKE-UP TEST!
PAUSE
ピタッ

FWAH
ド
CRICK
コキッ
MEH, IT WAS LIKE A LIGHT WARM-UP!

...
WELL, THEN! LET'S HURRY UP AND SWITCH BACK!
STEP
すた
すた
STEP
GEEZ...
SHE'S GOT SOME BALLS, SAYING THAT IN MY BODY!

The Next Day.
OH, URARA-CHAN!
WE HEARD FROM THE TEACHER!
!
...
THEY SAID THAT YOU CAUGHT THE PEEPERS!
DASH
DASH
DASH
ドドドドドド
HUH?
WE HEARD YOU TIED THOSE THREE CREEPS UP,
AND HANDED THEM OVER TO THE TEACHER!!
CHATTER
わい
THAT IS, LIKE, SO COOL! ♥
WEREN'T YOU SCARED?!
わい
CHATTER
わい
CHATTER
わい
CHATTER

UH...
UH-HUH...
Staffroom
職員室
STELLAR JOB, YAMADA!
A TRUE MIRACLE, I MUST SAY!
!
THAT GIRL...
追試問題
99
99
99
99
99
SHE DIDN'T HOLD BACK, DID SHE?!

OH, WELL!
AWESOME!
CAN'T COMPLAIN!

Student Council Meeting Room
生徒会室
AND SO...

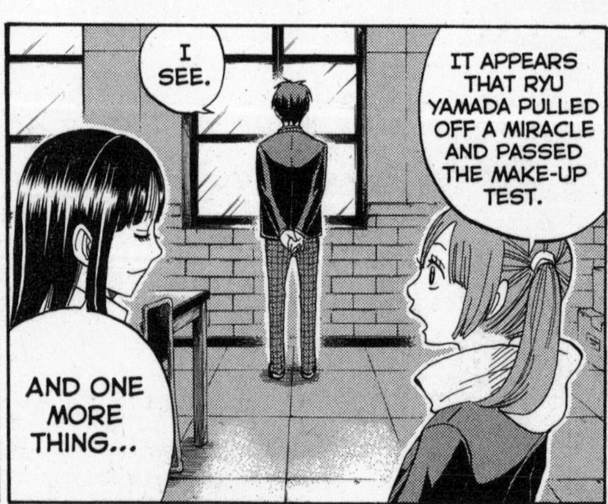
IT APPEARS THAT RYU YAMADA PULLED OFF A MIRACLE AND PASSED THE MAKE-UP TEST.
I SEE.
AND ONE MORE THING...

THANKS TO URARA SHIRAISHI,
THE ONES WHO WERE BEHIND THE PEEP PHOTOS HAVE BEEN CAUGHT.

WHAT?!
URARA? YOU MEAN THAT ANTI-SOCIAL STUDENT WHO GETS THE HIGHEST MARKS?!
TELL ME ABOUT IT!
FIRST YAMADA, THEN THIS! WHAT'S THE WORLD COMING TO?
HMM...
にっこぉ
SMILE
WELL, AT ANY RATE!
TURN
くるっ
WE ALL HAVE LESS WORK NOW, AND THAT'S ALWAYS A GOOD THING!

TRUE, TRUE!
CLATTER
ガタッ
HOW ABOUT WE HAVE OUR SNACKS EARLY TODAY? ♥
CLICK
CLACK
カツ
コツ
?

SHUT!
HUH? IS HE GOING HOME ALREADY?
I GUESS HE DIDN'T NEED A SNACK!
UH...DID YOU SEE THAT... JUST NOW?!
MIYAMURA WAS ACTUALLY SMILING, Y'KNOW?!
HMPH... YAMADA AND SHIRAISHI, HUH?
GRIN
THERE'S SOMETHING INTERESTING ABOUT THOSE TWO!!
Suzaku High School: 2nd Year
TORANOSUKE MIYAMURA

CHAPTER 3: I don't hate strong women.

WHAT?!
STARE
ボー
YOU HAVE A PHYSICS QUESTION?!

YES. IT'S ABOUT THE EXPERIMENT WE DID IN CLASS.
OH, OHH...
MY WORD, YAMADA! YOU'VE BEEN STUDYING REALLY HARD!
IT'S LMOST LIKE I DON'T KNOW YOU!

SIR... CAN YOU JUST ANSWER MY QUESTION?
OH... RIGHT, SORRY.
SNICKER! THAT STUPID TEACHER OESN'T EVEN KNOW IT'S SHIRAISHI INSIDE THAT BODY!

BAM
MAN, IS SHE FUN TO WATCH OR WHAT?!
URARA-CHAN!!
!
LET'S EAT LUNCH TOGETHER, GIRL!
GUESS WHAT?
I PACKED SANDWICHES FOR LUNCH TODAY!
CHATTER
ER... UH...
CHATTER
AND I BROUGHT TONS OF FRUIT!
AND I BROUGHT BEEF ON RICE! ♥
CHATTER
LET'S ALL SHARE!
A-ARE YOU SURE?
OF COURSE!
WE MADE TOO MUCH, Y'KNOW?
WAIT A SEC...! THIS WHOLE TIME I'VE BEEN FEELING IT...

BREASTS...
SQUISH
SQUISH
...RUBBING UP AGAINST ME!!

SIGH...
AHAHA
AHAHA

GUESS A GIRL'S WORLD AIN'T SO BAD...!!

LET'S GO TO THE CLASS-ROOM!
O-OKAY!

I GOTTA SAY...
SHIRAISHI MIGHT HAVE A POINT!

Five hours earlier (8 am)
CHIRP
CHIRP
OUR WHOLE WORLD HAS CHANGED, WOULDN'T YOU SAY?

?
YOU'VE NOTICED, HAVEN'T YOU?
THE EFFECT THAT THIS PERSONALITY SWAP HAS HAD ON OUR SCHOOL LIFE?

YOU GOT A GOOD SCORE ON YOUR TEST...
CHATTER
...AND I'VE MADE FRIENDS.

IT LOOKS LIKE SWITCHING BODIES WITH EACH OTHER
ENDED UP BENEFITING BOTH OF US, AFTER ALL!
I SEE.

BUT THE BIGGEST CHANGE OF ALL IS...

SCHOOL GOT A WHOLE LOT MORE FUN...!
TRUE!
SHE HAS A POINT!
STAND
THEN, HOW 'BOUT THIS?
TODAY, WHY DON'T WE...
...SWITCH BODIES UNTIL THE END OF THE SCHOOL DAY?!

2-B
WHAT A SPREAD!
MUNCH MUNCH
ガツガツ
GOBBLE GOBBLE GOBBLE
ばくばくばく
DO GIRLS REALLY EAT ALL THIS AWESOME FOOD EVERY DAY?!
MAN, THIS ISN'T FAIR AT ALL!
URARA-CHAN, I NEVER THOUGHT YOU'D HAVE SUCH A HEARTY APPETITE!
IT'S RE-FRESHING TO WATCH!
SCARF SCARF
FUNNY... NO ONE SUSPECTS ANYTHING.
THEN AGAIN, WHY WOULD THEY?
SHIRAI-SHI-SAN IS OVER THERE!
WHO WOULD EVEN GET THE IDEA...
STAND
...THAT THE TWO OF US HAVE SWITCHED PLACES?!

HEY, SHIRAISHI!
BEEN AWHILE...!
!
SORRY TO BUG YOU DURING LUNCH...
UT CAN I BORROW OU FOR A SEC?
THAT'S MIYAMURA-KUN, FROM STUDENT COUNCIL!
HE'S A BIT SCARY, BUT HE'S SO COOL!
...
OH, SHOOT.
O THIS GUY KNOWS HIRAISHI...?!

TORANOSUKE MIYAMURA... HE'S PRETTY WELL-KNOWN WITHIN MY CROWD.
SO HOW COME HE KNOWS AN HONOR STUDENT LIKE SHIRAISHI?

HEY, MIYAMUR KUN!
WHAT DO YOU PLAN ON DOING OUTSIDE WITH URARA-CHAN?
GIGGLE
...
SHUT YOUR TRAP. AS STUDENT COUNCIL VICE-PRESIDENT, I JUST NEED A WORD WITH URARA SHIRAISHI!
SINCE SHE HAS THE HIGHEST GRADES IN OUR YEAR!

OH...SO THAT'S WHAT THIS IS ABOUT.
THK
CLA-
THEN I GUESS I CAN'T TURN HIM DOWN!

WHY, SURE!
TURN
LET'S GO, SHALL WE? ♥

...OKAY.
SO WHAT DID YOU WANT TO TALK ABOUT?

I HEARD THAT YOU GAVE THOSE CHANGE-ROOM PERVS A REAL BEATING!
NEVER PEGGED YOU FOR THAT KIND OF GIRL!

JOLT
OH NO... HE ISN'T ONTO ME, IS HE?!

BUT THERE'S NO WAY HE WOULD SUSPECT WE SWITCHED BODIES...
OH, GOLLY! WHAT CAN I SAY? I SLIPPED AND MY FISTS JUST...HIT THEM! ♥
WIGGLE
WIGGLE
SO THEN, WHAT THE HELL DOES HE WANT?!

OH?
LEER
ぬっ
WELL, I DON'T HATE STRONG WOMEN.
YIKES!
O-OF...
OF COURSE YOU DON'T...
DOES HE...
OHH... HEH...
SLIDE
スススス
...HAVE A THING FOR SHIRAISHI...?!
BY THE WAY...YOU REMEMBER OUR PROMISE?
UH... THAT PROMISE?!
WHAT'S HE TALKING ABOUT?!
DON'T TELL ME YOU FORGOT...
ポリッ
SCRATCH

YOU SAID THAT...
YOU'D GO ON A *DATE* WITH ME, TODAY!
ARE YOU SERIOUS?!
SHE DID?!
GLOOM
ズーーン…
DAMN YOU, SHIRAI-SHI!
YOU NEVER TOLD ME ANY-THING ABOUT THIS!
AND WITH MIYAMURA AROUND, IT'S NOT LIKE I CAN JUST GO BACK!
WHY DO I HAVE TO GO ON A DATE WITH A DUDE?!

ISN'T THAT MIYAMURA FROM SUZAKU HIGH?!
YOU'RE RIGHT! LET'S SAY SOME-THING TO HIM!
HEY THERE! WHERE ARE YOU GOING?!
SCHWIP
NONE OF YOUR BUSINESS.
HE IS SOOO COOL!!!
SQUEAL
キャーッ
WHAT PART OF HIM EXACTLY?!
MAN, I NEVER GET A BREAK!
THAT HEAD CAN'T GET ANY BIGGER, CAN IT?!
FEH!
NOT A FAN OF THIS GUY AT ALL!
BY THE WAY, I HEARD A RUMOR THAT'S BEEN GOING AROUND...

SO IT SEEMS YOU'RE PRETTY CLOSE WITH YAMADA THESE DAYS?
JOLT
HUH?!
WH-WHAT DO YOU MEAN "CLOSE"?
?
UH, IF ANYTHING, IT'S THE EXACT OPPOSITE!
TH-THAT RUMOR REALLY, JUST... PISSES ME OFF!
OH?
I FIGURED AS MUCH.
I MEAN, A TOP STUDENT LIKE YOU...
AND A PUNK LIKE YAMADA...
YOU GUYS WOULD HAVE NOTHING IN COMMON!
HEY, MAN...
YOU TRYIN' TO SAY SOME-THING?
TWITCH
WHADDA WE HAVE HERE?

FWAH
YOU'RE...
URARA SHIRAISHI, AREN'TCHA?!
GAH!
THEY'RE THE PEEP PHOTOG-RAPHERS FROM BEFORE!!
WHAT ARE THEY DOING HERE?!
HAVIN' FUN ON YOUR DATE YER NOT GETTIN' OFF THE HOOK THAT EASY!
WE GOT KICKED OUT OF SCHOOL 'CAUSE OF YOU!!
...
WHO WERE THE ONES PEEPING IN THE FIRST PLACE?!
THESE CLOWNS! WHAT A PAIN!

GRAB
がしっ
EEEK! SAVE ME, MIYAMURA-KUN!
SQUISH
THOSE BAD GUYS ARE TRYING TO HURT ME AGAIN!
...I GOT THIS.
LEAVE IT TO ME!
YOU GO AND HIDE, OKAY?
CRACK
SWISH
ささっ
OKAY!

SWEET! PIECE OF CAKE!
IS HE FOR REAL?
SSSSSSH
シュウウウウウ
DUDE BLOWS, MAN!
NO-WAY!!
MIYAMURA'S WEAK AS HELL!!

MAN... SO HE WAS PUTTING ON A TOUGH ACT ALL ALONG...
STAND
OH WELL, I GUESS I GOTTA CLEAN 'EM UP MYSELF!
IT'S A GOOD THING MIYAMURA'S OUT COLD!
SMIRK
YER NEXT!
DASH
ARGH!
URARA SHIRAI-SHI!!
THWACK
!

TURN
WHAT THE?!
KA-
HAI-YAH!!
POW
A...
A ROUND-HOUSE KICK?!

CRASH
HELL YEAH!
TWO MORE TO GO!
UH...
WHOOSH
THEY'RE ALREADY DOWN FOR THE COUNT...
I KNEW IT!
CRUSH
THAT ROUND-HOUSE KICK...
I'VE SEEN IT BEFORE!

BOOM
I STARTED GETTING SUSPICIOUS AFTER HEARING ABOUT THE PEEPERS!
MIYA-MURA...!
NOT ONLY DID I NOT MAKE A DATE WITH SHIRAISHI...
BUT WE DON'T EVEN KNOW EACH OTHER!
YOU GAVE YOURSELF AWAY...
POINT
RUMBLE
RUMBLE

RUMBLE
YOU'RE YAMADA, AREN'T YOU?!

WH-WHAT?!
H-HOW DOES THAT MAKE ANY SENSE?!
M-ME? YAMADA?!
WHY WOULD I BE IN SHIRAI-
OH...
WHOOPS.
GRAB
LISTEN UP!
I HAVE A FAVOR TO ASK YOU...!

Yamada-kun and the Seven Witches
YOU SWITCH BODIES AFTER YOU KISS...?!
Archives
資料室
YEAH... SHIRAISHI AND I HAD A BIT OF AN ACCIDENT.
AND THAT'S HOW WE ENDED UP IN EACH OTHER'S BODIES...!
...OH? ALL FROM SOMETHING SO SIMPLE, HUH?
ERM, SHOULDN'T YOU BE MORE SURPRISED?
I WAS TRYING TO TRICK YOU INTO TELLING THE TRUTH
DAMN...
DON'T THINK SO LIGHTLY OF THE STUDENT COUNCIL EXEC!
BUT WHO KNEW YOU COULD ACTUALLY SWITCH BODIES?!
THIS IS BAD!
THAT WAS SUPPOSED TO BE A SECRET BETWEEN SHIRAISHI AND ME!

SO...
WHAT'S THIS FAVOR YOU WANT?
THERE'S SOMETHING I WANT YOU TO HELP ME CHECK OUT!
AND IT'S SOMETHING YOU CAN ONLY DO AS YOU ARE NOW!
OU MEAN, ME IN HIRAISHI'S BODY?
THAT'S EXACTLY WHAT I MEAN!
School Year Newsletters
学年だより
College Entrance Reports
進路調査書
IN OTHER WORDS...

FWP
College Entrance Reports
進路調査書
2-B
I WANT TO KNOW WHAT'S REALLY GOING ON IN URARA SHIRAISHI'S PRIVATE LIFE!!

CHAPTER 4: She's an E-cup!

FIRST, I WANT YOU TO TAKE A LOOK AT THIS.
College Entrance Reports
進路調査書
2-B

THIS IS FROM APRIL OF THIS YEAR...
IT HAS THE CAREER ASSESSMENT SURVEYS THAT WE TOOK RIGHT AFTER ENTERING INTO SECOND YEAR.
HMM...

WHICH, BY THE WAY,
YOU STILL AVEN'T URNED IN, AMADA!
URK!

FLIP
HAVE A LOOK AT URARA SHIRAI-SHI'S REPORT.

BECAUSE OF HER CAREER ASSESS-MENT...
THE STUDENT COUNCIL HAS A PROBLEM NOW.

!

WHAT?
Career Assessment Survey
Year: 2 B (37) Urara Shiraishi
1. Do you have plans to go to college?
Yes
No
SHE ISN'T GOING TO COLLEGE?!
BUT SHE STUDIES SO MUCH! WHAT A WEIRDO!
I KNOW, RIGHT?

SHE'S THE HIGHEST-ACHIEVING STUDENT IN OUR SCHOOL BAR NONE,
SO WHY ISN'T SHE PLANNING TO GO TO COLLEGE?
IT'S A LOSS FOR THE WHOLE SCHOOL!

WHO KNOWS? SHE PROB-ABLY HAS STUFF GOING ON IN HER LIFE...
YOU KNOW, LIKE FAMILY ISSUES.
HER GUARDIANS WANT HER TO GO TO COLLEGE, TOO!
REALLY?!

HMM... THEN DOES THAT MEAN...
...THAT SHE HERSELF DOESN'T WANT TO GO TO COLLEGE?

THAT'S EXACTLY IT! THE TEACHERS EVEN ASKED US AT THE STUDENT COUNCIL TO TALK SOME SENSE INTO HER...
BUT SHE VOULDN'T ISTEN...

SO WE'VE GOT NOTHING! WE WON'T GET ANYWHERE JUST BY WATCHING HER AT SCHOOL.
AND IT'S NOT LIKE I CAN MEDDLE IN HER PERSONAL LIFE.
LIKE IF SHE'S PURSUING A "DREAM" OR SOME-THING?
...YEAH, LIKE THAT.

WHATEVER IT TAKES, I'M GONNA FIND OUT WHY SHIRAISHI DOESN'T WANT TO GO TO COLLEGE!
THEN, I'M GONNA USE THAT TO CONVINCE HER TO GO!
BAM
HE'S MORE PAS-SIONATE THAN I THOUGHT!
SO, THAT'S...

...WHERE I COME IN, HUH?
YOU CATCH ON FAST!

ALL RIGHT, THEN! I'LL DO YOU THAT FAVOR!
BUT ON ONE CONDITION...
DON'T TELL SHIRAISHI...
THAT YOU KNOW ABOUT THE SECRET, OKAY?!

?
'CAUSE I PROMISED HER I WOULDN'T TELL ANYBODY...
...HMPH.
AGREED.
PHEW!
ホッ
OKAY, THEN! HURRY UP AND COME WITH ME!

白石
SHIRAISHI
LOOKS LIKE THIS IS IT!
SHIRAISHI'S HOUSE!
!
JUST YOUR AVERAGE, ORDINARY HOUSE...
HUGE, THOUGH.
A-ARE YOU REALLY PLANNING ON JUST BREAKING IN?!
DON'T TELL ME YOU'RE GETTING COLD FEET NOW!
BY THE WAY, IF WE RUN INTO ANYONE, I'M YOUR BOYFRIEND, GOT IT?
WE GOTTA GET OUR STORIES STRAIGHT!
YOU? ET'S JUST KEEP IT S CLASS-MATES.

SHIRAISHI'S HOUSE, HUH...? WITH ALL THE BODY-SWITCHIN WE'VE DONE....
I REALLY DON'T KNOW HER ALL THAT WELL, DO I?!
RUSTLE RUSTLE
OH, WELL! I GUESS I'LL TAKE THIS OPPOR-TUNITY
TO GET TO KNOW HER BETTER, THEN...!
JUST TO B CLEAR...IF SHIRAISHI CATCHES ME DOING THIS...
YOU DON'T KNOW HOW MUCH TROUBLE WE'RE GOING TO BE IN!
SO BE EXTREMELY CAREFUL WHEN WE—
RATTLE
RATTLE
IT WON'T OPEN!
YOU'RE NOT EVEN LISTENING, ARE YOU?!
WHAT THE HELL ARE YOU GONNA DO IF SOMEONE'S IN THERE?! THEY'LL GET SUSPICIOUS!!
IT'S NOT LIKE YOU CAN SNEAK INTO YOUR OWN HOUSE, EITHER! THAT'S EVEN MORE SUSPICIOUS!
GASP!
YOU GOT A POINT!

KER-CHAK
SQUEEEEAK
I'M...
UH, HOOOME...

SILENCE
LOOKS LIKE NO ONE'S HERE...

JOLT
KYAAA!
HISS!
SHE HAS A BLACK CAT?
I'M CARED OF CATS!

HM...
IT'S A PRETTY...
NORMAL HOUSE...
HEY, YAMADA!
UP HERE!
STEP
POINT POINT
?
うらら☆のへや
Urara's Room
OOH!
SO SHIRAISHI'S SECRETS ARE IN THERE!
GULP
KER-CHAK
THIS IS THE HONOR STUDENT THAT KISSED ME LIKE IT WAS NOTHING!
THERE'S NO WAY THIS IS GONNA BE JUST ANY OLD ROOM!

FWAAHH
!
IT'S ACTUALLY ...
A PRETTY NORMAL-LOOKING GIRL'S ROOM!
SMELLS LIKE SHIRAISHI!
SNIFF SNIFF
HMM...I NEVER THOUGHT SHE'D HAVE ALL THESE CUTE THINGS.
LET ME BE CLEAR, MIYAMURA! DON'T YOU DARE MESS UP HER STUFF, GOT IT?
'CAUSE IF SHE NOTICES, I'M THE ONE SHE'S GONNA SUSPECT!

ARE WE CLEAR?!
SHE'S AN E-CUP.
I'M NOT KIDDING AROUND HERE!!
I'M TELLING YOU NOT TO TOUCH HER STUFF, AND YOU'RE RIFLING THROUGH HER UNDERWEAR DRAWER?!!
I JUST OPENED IT AND THERE IT WAS.
AREN'T YOU LUCKY?! NOW PUT THOSE BACK WHERE THEY WERE, DAMN IT!
HEY YAMADA, YOU DON'T NOTICE ANYTHING ABOUT THAT MOUNTAIN OF WHITE UNDERWEAR?
?

THUD
WE CAN'T LET THE SMALLEST CLUE SLIP BY US!
HEY! FOLD THEM NICELY, WILL YA?!
GIRLS WHO LIKE WHITE UNDERWEAR TEND TO BE GENTLE!
AND WHAT DOES THAT HAVE TO DO WITH HER NOT GOING TO COLLEGE?
SNAP
DAMN IT! YOU WANT US TO GET CAUGHT?!

LEMME SEE...
FWUM
ACK! WHAT ARE YOU GETTING IN THE BED FOR?!
I'M CHECKING FOR CLUES.
RUSTLE
C'MON! EVERYONE KNOWS SECRETS ARE GENERALLY KEPT AROUND THE BED!

NO LUCK.
DID YOU HAVE TO JUMP INSIDE THE COVERS IN THE FIRST PLACE?!

BAF
BAF
DAMN IT! YOU CAN'T JUST LEAVE THE BED UNMADE!!
HMM...
THERE ARE ONLY SCHOOL TEXTBOOKS AND REFERENCE BOOKS IN HER BOOKSHELF...
AND HER DESK DRAWERS ARE MOSTLY JUST STATIONERY...

STRANGE...
NONE OF THIS HELPS US AT ALL...!
NOW WHY THE HELL DOES SHIRAISHI NOT WANT TO GO TO COLLEGE?
....I GUESS IT'S COME TO THIS.
THERE'S ONLY ONE OTHER THING I CAN THINK OF!
ばっ
HEY, YAMADA!
GRAB
ガ
LEMME SEE YOUR BODY!
HEY!! WHAT ARE YOU DOING?!
FLAIL
はた
はた
FLAIL
THERE'S GOTTA BE SOME CHRONIC ILLNESS SHIRAISHI IS HIDING FROM HER PARENTS!
ARE YOU NUTS?!
SHE'S HEALTHY!! THERE'S NOTHING WRONG WITH HER–

BODY?!!

RUMBLE
OH MY GOD!!! WE ARE SOOO SORRY!!!
RUMBLE
L-LET ME JUST SAY... NONE OF THIS WAS MY IDEA, OKAY?!
MIYAMURA WAS THE ONE WHO SAW YOUR UNDERWEAR AND SLEPT IN YOUR BED!!
UH, WELL, IT WAS THIS GUY WHO RUBBED YOUR BREAST AGAINST MY ARM!
GRAB
SQUISH
IDIOT! YOU WANT HER TO GET MORE PISSED THAN SHE ALREADY IS?!
I DIDN'T ASK FOR YOUR EXCUSES.
RIGHT!! SORRY!!

YOU DIDN'T SHOW UP AT THE TIME WE AGREED ON, SO...
I STARTED TO GET WORRIED.

AND THEN, I FIND MY ROOM RAN-SACKED...
JOLT
ギクッ
AND LEARN THAT MIYAMURA-KUN KNOWS OUR SECRET.

I...
I SCREWED UP.

IT'S FINE. I THOUGHT THIS WAS GONNA HAPPEN, ANYWAY.
...

BY THE WAY, WHAT WERE YOU DOING IN MY ROOM?

UH, SO I HEARD FROM THIS GUY THAT YOU'RE NOT GONNA GO TO COLLEGE, SO...
WE WERE TRYING TO FIND OUT WHY.

ALTHOUGH WE DIDN'T END UP FINDING ANYTHING...
WILL YOU STAY OUT OF OTHER PEOPLE'S HOUSES?
YES, MA'AM!!

B-BUT HEY,
WHY DON'T YOU WANT TO GO TO COLLEGE?
I MEAN, YOU CAN AT LEAST TELL US THAT, RIGHT?

BECAUSE...
I HATE SCHOOL.
!

I WAS NEVER ABLE TO MAKE FRIENDS,
AND WHEN I THOUGHT I DID, I GOT BULLIED.
IF STUDYING IS ALL SCHOOL IS FOR,
THEN I JUST DON'T SEE THE POINT.
THAT'S WHY I DON'T WANT TO GO TO COLLEGE!
OH...
すっ STAND
BUT... THAT WAS BACK WHEN I FILLED OUT THE CAREER ASSESSMENT SURVEY...
HUH?
!
THINGS ARE DIFFERENT NOW...
WHOAAA...!
?
SO...

IF YOU GO, THEN I'LL GO, TOO!
SHUT
ぽか UHHH... ん
...YAMADA, YOU'RE GETTING EXTRA LESSONS EVERY DAY, STARTING TOMORROW!
WHAT?!

Yamada-kun AND THE Seven Witches

CHAPTER 5: Whaddya say we do this together?

Student Council Meeting Room
生徒会室
URARA SHIRAISHI'S THINKING OF GOING TO COLLEGE?!
BLUB BLUB
...YUP!

TH... THAT'S AMAZING, MIYAMURA-KUN!
A JOB WELL DONE!
CLATTER
I CAN'T BELIEVE IT...!
ALL OF US ON THE STUDENT COUNCIL HAD JUST ABOUT GIVEN UP ON THAT!
B-BUT...HOW ON EARTH DID YOU DO IT...?!
KER-CHAK
NONE OF YOUR BUSINESS!
SHUT
GRR!
WHAT'S HIS PROBLEM?!
YOU KNOW, TORANOSUKE-KUN'S STOCK IS GONNA GO WAY UP WITH THIS!
YOU CAN'T SLACK OFF EITHER, NENE-SAN!

I KNOW THAT!
Suzaku High: 2nd Year
Student Council Vice President
NENE ODAGIRI
2-B
CLATTER
ざわ ざわ
CLATTER
ざわ ざわ
CLATTER
ざわ ざわ
Lovely Milk

IT'S BEEN A WEEK SINCE SHIRAISHI AGREED TO GO TO COLLEGE...
SINCE THEN, WE HAVEN'T SWITCHED BODIES ONCE...
AND WE'VE BEEN SPENDING OUR DAYS ON OUR OWN.

THESE DAYS, SHIRAISHI...
URARA-CHAN, IT MUST BE SO NICE TO HAVE LONG LASHES!
AND YOUR HAIR'S SO SILKY!
...HAS RAPIDLY BECOME THE POPULAR KID IN SCHOOL.
AND AS FOR ME...
YOU DON'T HAVE ANY QUESTIONS FOR ME?
I'VE BECOME POPULAR, TOO... WITH THE TEACHERS.
NO! I REALLY DON'T!

AND SO...
WITH THE TWO OF US BEING BUSY WITH OUR OWN LIVES AT SCHOOL...

PASS
ス...
THERE HAS BEEN ABSOLUTELY NO CHANCE FOR US TO SWITCH PLACES.
I WENT TO DISNEY-LAND YESTER-DAY!
REALLY? WHO'D YA GO WITH?

...AH WELL,
IT LOOKS LIKE SHE'S ENJOYING SCHOOL A LOT MORE NOW, SO...
I GUESS THERE'S NO NEED TO SWITCH BODIES ANYMORE...

WHOA! YAMADA'S WISTFULLY REMINISCING!
CLATTER
ACK!
MI-MIYAMURA!!
HOW LONG HAVE YOU BEEN SITTING THERE?!
FOR AS LONG AS YOU'VE HAD THAT BORING LOOK ON YOUR FACE.

HUH?! BORING? WHO'RE YOU CALLING "BORING"
HEY, I DON'T BLAME YOU!
EVER SINCE YOU STOPPED SWITCHING BODIES, THINGS HAVE BEEN BORING FOR ME, TOO!
HUH ...?
THAT'S WHY I HAVE A PROPOSAL FOR THE BOTH OF YOU!

URARA-CHAN!
MIYAMURA-KUN FROM THE STUDENT COUNCIL IS CALLING FOR YOU AGAIN!
?
AGAIIIN?
BEING FIRST IN THE CLASS MUST BE TOUGH!

WELL, IF IT ISN'T MIYAMUUU!
HMPH!
MIYA-WHO?

C'MERE

!

Do Not Use
使用禁止
SO...
TURN キョロ
TURN キョロ
WHAT'S THIS "PROPOSAL" YOU WERE TALKING ABOUT?
DID YOU HAVE TO BRING US TO THIS DUSTY PLACE?
IT LOOKS LIKE A CLUBROOM THAT ISN'T BEING USED...
RIGHT! THAT'S EXACTLY WHAT IT IS!
I AM OFFERING THIS CLUBROOM TO YOU GUYS!
?!!

THIS CLUBROOM WAS ORIGINALLY USED BY THE SUPERNATURAL STUDIES CLUB,
BUT DUE TO A LACK OF MEMBERS, THE CLUB IS CURRENTLY INACTIVE.
RIP
Supernatural Studies Club
超常現象研究部
SO I THOUGHT I WOULD LET YOU TWO USE IT AS YOU LIKE!

US?! WHAT'S THAT SUPPOSED TO MEAN?
ISN'T IT OBVIOUS?
Supernatural Studies Club
超常現象研究部
THE TWO OF YOU NEED A PLACE TO KISS AT SCHOOL!

!
UH... HUHH?!
NOW THAT SHIRAISHI IS SO POPULAR,
I'M SURE IT ISN'T EASY TO KISS HER ON SCHOOL GROUNDS!
WHISPER WHISPER
YOU WANTED A PLACE LIKE THIS, AM I RIGHT?
C'MON, MAN...
HOW-EVER!

IN EXCHANGE, YOU HAVE TO JOIN THE SUPERNATURAL STUDIES CLUB!!
MAKES SENSE, DOESN'T IT? THE CLUBROOM IS FOR CLUB MEMBERS ONLY!
!
WHAT IS THIS SUPER-NATURAL WHATCHA-MA-CALL-IT?!
THIS CLUB FOCUSES ON PHENOMENA THAT CAN'T BE EXPLAINED THROUGH SCIENCE!
AND THE STUDY OF IT, TO BE EXACT!
PERFECT FOR THE TWO OF YOU, WOULDN'T YOU SAY?
IN ANY CASE, I'M NOT GONNA FORCE YOU TO JOIN THE CLUB,
SINCE THAT'S NOT WHAT CLUB ACTIVITIES ARE ABOUT, ANYWAY!
RATTLE RATTLE
ガラ ガラ
YOU TALK IT OVER WITH EACH OTHER, THEN GET BACK TO ME!
LOCK
JUST LETTING YOU KNOW, I ALREADY JOINED THIS CLUB LAST YEAR, TO KEEP IT ALIVE.

WELL, THEN! I'LL BE WAITING FOR YOUR FAVORABLE ANSWER!
WHO WOULD'VE THOUGHT HE WOULD BE IN THE UPERNATURAL STUDIES CLUB?!

...

A CLUB, HUH? I DON'T KNOW...

UHH... RIGHT?!
AND I'M TOTALLY NOT INTO THAT KIND OF STUFF...

...YEAH.
I HAVE STUDIES TO DO, TOO...

SHUT
Comprehensive Collection of Physics Problems
BUT...

JOINING A CLUB DOES SOUND LIKE FUN!

HEY! IT'S URARA-CHAN!
!

C'MON! LUNCH IS ALMOST OVER!
THINGS ARE FINE THIS WAY...
EVERY-THING GO ALL RIGHT?
YUP.
BESIDES, THERE'S NO REASON FOR US TO SWITCH BODIES ANYMORE...

THE WORLDS WE LIVE IN WERE TOO DIFFERENT TO BEGIN WITH!
...AND THAT GUY FROM BEFORE ...
OH GOD, NO!
HEY, SHIRAISHI!

I'M GONNA JOIN THAT CLUB, AFTER ALL!
SO...
WHADDYA SAY WE DO THIS TOGETHER?!
WHAT?
IT'S YAMADA ...

OKAY!

Supernatural Studies Club
超常現象研究部
...ALL RIGHT, THEN!
BADUMP!!
UGH! A SPIDER WEB?!
STICKY
ベと〜っ
THE SUPER-NATURAL STUDIES CLUB RESUMES TODAY!
THE PRESIDENT OF THE CLUB WILL BE SHIRAISHI-SAN!
HUH? ME?
I WILL BE VICE-PRESI-DENT!
AND YAMADA, YOU'LL BE THE COMMON-ER!
THE COM-MON-ER?!

JUST SO YOU KNOW, I WAS THE ONE WHO OFFERED YOU THIS NICE PLACE!
SO IT'D BE GREAT IF FROM HERE ON OUT, YOU GUYS COULD LISTEN TO THE STUDENT COUNCIL FROM TIME TO TIME!
WHAT A BOTHER!
TCH!
HEY!

WELL, TO START OFF OUR CLUB ACTIVITIES...
I HAVE A QUESTION I'D LIKE TO CLEAR UP...
?

YAMADA AND SHIRAISHI-SAN...
HAVE EITHER OF YOU EVER KISSED ANYONE ELSE BEFORE?
CLATTER
...URK!
WHAT KIND OF QUESTION IS THAT?!

NO.
HUH?
SO, YAMADA WAS YOUR FIRST...
AND HOW 'BOUT YOU, YAMADA?

SH-SHIRAISHI...
...WAS MY FIRST, TOO.

HMM...SO IT WAS TH FIRST TIM FOR BOTH YOU...
THEN THERE IS A POSSIBILITY...
?
ニヤリ
SMIRK
YOU GUYS FOUND OUT BY CHANCE THAT YOU COULD SWITCH BODIES AFTER KISSING...
SO THE SAME THING COULD HAPPEN WITH SOMEONE ELSE...
WHICH MEANS!
BAM

YOU CAN SWITCH BODIES WITH OTHER PEOPLE, TOO!

MY NAME IS RYU YAMADA.
THROUGH AN UNUSUAL EVENT THAT LED TO ME KISSING URARA SHIRAISHI, THE SMARTEST STUDENT IN MY CLASS,
WE GAINED THE POWER TO SWITCH BODIES WITH EACH OTHER.

TORANOSUKE MIYAMURA, THE VICE-PRESIDENT OF THE STUDENT COUNCIL,
DISCOVERED OUR SECRET!

THROUGH MIYAMURA'S OFFER, THE TWO OF US ENDED UP JOINING THE ONCE-DEFUNCT SUPERNATURAL STUDIES CLUB.
Vice-President
President
Commoner
HEY!
AND THE CLUB'S FIRST TOPIC OF DISCUSSION IS...
Supernatural Studies Club
超常現象研究部

Yamada-kun and the Seven Witches

WE CAN SWITCH BODIES WITH ANYONE WE KISS?! C'MON, MAN!
HE DOES RAISE A GOOD POINT...
ACK! BUT STILL...
IT'S ALWAYS GOOD TO TRY NEW THINGS!

SO HOW 'BOUT IT, SHIRAISHI-SAN?
WANNA GIVE ME A KISS...?
GRIP
BAM
?!!

CHAPTER 6: I'm not a guinea pig, y'know?!

どーーん
BADUM
DEFINITELY NOT GONNA HAPPEN!

!
PHEW!
ホッ
D-DAMN IGHT IT'S NOT!

IT'S NOT EVEN GUARANTEED THAT YOU'LL SWITCH BODIES IN THE FIRST PLACE...
SHE'S NOT GONNA KISS YOU THAT EASILY!
FINE. I'LL SETTLE FOR YAMADA, THEN.
HEY! SHOULDN'T YOU BE EELING FROM HE SHOCK OF SHIRAISHI TURNING YOU DOWN RIGHT ABOUT NOW?!

AND WHAT DO YOU MEAN YOU'LL SETTLE FOR ME?!
THAT'S TWO GUYS KISSING, OKAY?!
SORRY, MAN, BUT THAT'S JUST... GROSS!!
NOT REALLY.
HUH?
IF WE CAN SWITCH BODIES LIKE THIS, A KISS IS NO BIG DEAL!
C'MON, YAMADA-KUN, IT'S FOR THE CLUB!
DO YOUR BEST!
GRAB
DO MY BEST?! WHAT THE HELL DO YOU THINK THIS-
!
HEY! HOLD ON A MINUTE!
GLOW
GLOW
WHERE'D THIS MOOD LIGHTING COME FROM?!
HERE WE GO, YAMADA!
YANK

ぶ
SMOOCH
ちゅっ
ROLL
ゴロ
ROLL
ゴロ
ROLL
ゴロ
BLECH! ARGH!
YUCK!
ドサッ
THUD
!
!
?!!
WHAT THE HELL?!
I NEVER SAID I WAS GONNA DO ANYTHING, OKAY?!
ペッ
PTOO
ペッ
PTOO

WHOA...
!
WE REALLY SWITCHED ...?!!
?!!
SICK!
ZIP
ZIP
SO THIS IS YAMADA'S BODY!
シュ
SCHWIP
N-NO WAY...

THAT'S AMAZING! SO IT MIGHT BE THAT...
YOU CAN SWITCH WITH ANYONE JUST BY KISSING THEM...?!
H-HOW AM I SUPPOSED TO KNOW SOMETHING LIKE THAT?!
BUT...
THIS IS REALLY IYAMURA'S BODY, HUH...?
I KNOW IT'S OBVIOUS, BUT THIS BODY REALLY FEELS DIFFERENT FROM SHIRAISHI'S ...
GRIP
GRIP
IT'S EASIER TO MOVE IN THIS BODY...
...AND FLEXING THE MUSCLES FEELS DIFFERENT, TOO...
IT FEELS A LOT CLOSER TO MY OWN.
SHIRAISHI, WHEN I FIRST SWITCHED BODIES WITH YOU, I WAS SO FREAKED OUT I DIDN'T NOTICE ANYTHING...
BUT THE BODY FEELS TOTALLY DIFFERENT DEPENDING ON THE PERSON, Y'KNOW?
...OH.
SO HE HAS SOMETHING STRANGE STUCK TO HIS CROTCH, TOO?
YA THINK?! AND WHY ARE YOU SO INTO THAT?!
FWIP

HEY, THERE IS SOMETHING WEIRD STUCK TO HIS CROTCH!!
YOU DON'T HAVE TO GET IN THERE, DUDE!!

...UGH! WHATEVER, MAN!
NOW WE KNOW I CAN SWITCH BODIES WITH YOU, SO...
LET'S HURRY UP AND SWITCH BACK!!

GAK! WHERE'D HE GO?!

MIYAMURA-KUN SAID HE WAS GONNA TAKE A QUICK TOUR OF THE SCHOOL AND COME BACK.
HE WHAT?!

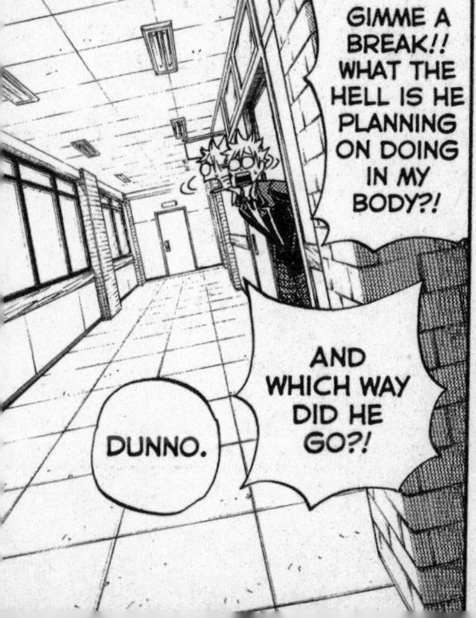
GIMME A BREAK!! WHAT THE HELL IS HE PLANNING ON DOING IN MY BODY?!
AND WHICH WAY DID HE GO?!
DUNNO.

DAMN THAT MIYAMURA!
GLANCE キョロ
GLANCE キョロ
DON'T TRY ANYTHING DUMB NOW...
EEEK! IT'S MIYAMURA-SENPAI!
OH MY GOD! HE'S SO COOL! ♥
!
HEY! DID HE JUST NOTICE US?!
EEK! SENPAI, LOOK OVER HERE!
TURN くるっ
'SUP!

TCH
THAT'S WEIRD. SENPAI DOESN'T HAVE HIS VIBE TODAY!
HE MUST BE TIRED.
IT'S MIYAMURA-KUN!
SQUEAL
SQUEAL
SQUEAL
DAMN IT...! THEY KEEP POPPING UP ONE AFTER ANOTHER...
IS THIS WHAT POPULAR KIDS PUT UP WITH...?!
I GOTTA FIND THIS GUY, FAST!
HEY, MIYAMURA!
!
HOLD ON A MINUTE!
?

IF I REMEMBER CORRECTLY, SHE'S... ON THE STUDENT COUNCIL LIKE MIYAMURA...
NENE ODAGIRI, WAS IT...?

THIS IS BAD...
SHE PROBABLY KNOWS MIYAMURA PRETTY WELL, THEN!!

YOU'RE REALLY PUSHING YOUR LUCK THESE DAYS, YOU KNOW?
N-NOT REALLY.
...OH, SO THESE TWO ARE ON BAD TERMS, HUH?!

I GUESS I'LL JUST GO WITH THE FLOW.
...SO? WHAT DO YOU WANT?
I HEARD FROM THE OTHER EXECS...
YOU STARTED UP THE SUPERNATURAL STUDIES CLUB AGAIN?

IT'S BECOME KIND OF A JOKE!
THE FACT THAT YOU'RE SO ATTACHED TO *THAT CLUB!*
?
I MEAN, WOULDN'T YOU AGREE?
LIKE, URARU SHIRAISHI IS ONE THING...

BUT A DOPE LIKE THAT YAMADA?
SNICKER
YOU'D GO SO LOW AS TO INVITE THE *SCHOOL'S DEAD WEIGHT!*

TWITCH
SAY THAT AGAIN?!

WHAT?
QUIVER
QUIVER
...NOTHIN'.

...WHAT-EVER.
CLICK
CLACK
WORK HARD ON YOUR POINTLESS LITTLE CLUB...

ス...
PASS
YOU'LL ONLY BE ABLE TO DO IT FOR SO LONG, ANYWAY..!!
STEP すた
STEP すた
HAT IS P WITH HER?!
BUT WHAT DID SHE MEAN...
WHEN SHE SAID MIYAMURA IS SO ATTACHED TO THE SUPERNATURAL STUDIES CLUB?
HEY, YAMADA!
MIYA-MURA, YOU!!
WHERE THE HELL HAVE YOU BE-
SHHH!
NOT RIGHT NOW!! THIS IS ERIOUS!!
THERE'S SOMETHING I REALIZED WHEN BEING IN YOUR BODY, YAMADA...
!

SHOCK
EVERYONE IN SCHOOL HATES YOU!!
IS THAT IT?!!
WAIT, YOU ALREAD KNEW!?
WHEREVER I GO, NO ONE TALKS TO ME, AND WHEN I TRY TO TALK TO THEM, THEY WON'T EVEN GIVE ME THE TIME OF DAY!
ARE YOU ALL RIGHT, MAN?!
SHADDUP! LEAVE IT ALONE, WILL YA?!
I SEE... I REALLY THOUGHT SOMETHING TERRIBLE HAPPENED, Y'KNOW?
WELL, THIS IS GETTING LAME, SO LET'S HEAD BACK, SHALL WE?
OH, SO YOU GET TO DECIDE THAT?!

Supernatural Studies Club
超常現象研究部
...AND SO...
AT THE VERY LEAST, WE FOUND OUT THAT YAMADA CAN SWITCH BODIES WITH SHIRAISHI-SAN AND ME...
YOU SURE SWITCHED BACK QUICKLY...
YOU THINK I COULD STAND ANY MORE OF THAT?!
BUT SERIOUSLY THOUGH, DOESN'T THAT MEAN YAMADA-KUN CAN SWITCH BODIES WITH ANYONE JUST BY KISSING THEM?!
HMM.
IF THAT'S TRUE... THEN THIS S A PRETTY BIG DEAL, ISN'T IT?
SLAM
OKAY! I GOT IT!
I'M GONNA BRING OVER A *GIRL WHO WILL KISS JUST ABOUT ANYONE!!*
BAM
THEN WE'LL KNOW YAMADA'S POWER FOR SURE, RIGHT?
YOU'RE A REAL IDIOT, Y'KNOW THAT?! THERE'S NO GIRL LIKE THAT OUT THERE!!
YEAH, THERE IS! IN CLASS D...
HOLD ON!

I'D RATHER WE NOT.
Classical Literature
古文
?
SHIRAISHI ...?

WHY NOT? WE NEED TO DO THIS EXPERIMENT, Y'KNOW?
AND I'M SAYING THAT WE DON'T.
...

WHAT'S UP WITH SHIRAISHI?
SHE SEEMED ALL INTERESTED IN MY POWER A MINUTE AGO...
COULD IT BE...
THAT SHE'S JEALOUS OF ME KISSING ANOTHER GIRL?
LISTEN, OKAY?
ガタ
CLATTER
THIS IS AN ORDER FROM THE PRESIDENT!

THE FACT THAT YAMADA-KUN HAS THE POWER TO SWITCH BODIES...
...WILL BE KEPT A SECRET THAT STAYS WITH US IN THIS CLUB...!!
?
I TOLD YOU BEFORE, DIDN'T I?
IF THIS GETS OUT TO THE SCHOOL, THINGS WILL GET MESSY...!
THAT'S WHY WE CAN'T LET ANYONE KNOW ABOUT THIS...!

GEEZ... SO THAT'S WHY?!!
COLLAPSE
HMM... THAT'S VERY TRUE...
THEN HOW 'BOUT THIS?
"ALWAYS KEEP THE SECRET!"
THIS WILL BE OUR CLUB'S RULE!
YOU'RE COOL WITH THAT, RIGHT, YAMADA?
YEAH, SURE!
AND WHEN IT COMES TO YOUR POWER, WE'L STUDY IT O A GRADUAL BASIS, THEN!
NICE! THIS IS STARTING TO FEEL LIKE A CLUB ACTIVITY!
Supernatu Studies Clu
BUT, C'MON! A RULE?
AS LONG AS WE DON'T TELL ANYONE, THE SECRET'S NOT GOING ANYWHERE!
AND IT'S NOT LIKE ANYONE'S GONNA ENTER A WEIRD, NO-NAME CLUB LIKE THIS!
I'M NOT A GUINEA PIG, Y'KNOW?!
THAT'S TRUE.
THEIR REPUTATION WOULD BE AT STAKE.
GLANCE
WHAT'S THAT SUPPOSED TO MEAN?!

UH, EXCUSE ME...?
!
I HEAR THAT THE SUPERNATURAL STUDIES CLUB HAS STARTED UP AGAIN...
IS THIS THE PLACE?
I...
WOULD LIKE TO JOIN YOUR CLUB...!!

Supernatural Studies Club
超常現象研究部
WHAAA?!!

DID YOU NOT HEAR ME?
I SAID I WANT TO JOIN THE SUPER-NATURAL STUDIES CLUB!
Suzaku High: 2nd Year
Miyabi Itou
IS SHE SERIOUS?! SHE WANTS TO JOIN THIS BEAT-DOWN CLUB?!
I MEAN, I CAN'T BE-LIEVE THAT SOMEONE ACTUALLY WANTS TO JOIN!!
WH-WHAT ARE WE GONNA DO?!
WHAT DO YOU MEAN, "WHAT ARE WE GONNA DO?" OUR SCHOOL HAS NO SYSTEM FOR REFUSING APPLICANTS.
WE HAVE NO CHOICE BUT TO LET HER JOIN...!!
Yamada-kun AND THE Seven Witches

CHAPTER 7: It's now or never!!

WHAT KIND OF SUPER-NATURAL STUDY ARE YOU GUYS DOING NOW?

STUDY? UH WELL...
I MEAN, WE JUST STARTED OUR CLUB NOT TOO LONG AGO Y'KNOW...
W-WE JUST JOINED, SO WE KNOW NOTHING ABOUT THE SUPER-NATURAL...

WHAT? ARE YOU GUYS FOR REAL?!

HUH ?!
NO PROBLEM! IN THAT CASE, LEAVE IT TO ME!

'CAUSE I HAVE THE POWER TO BEND SPOONS, Y'KNOW?!
!
WHOA.
YOU READY? WATCH CLOSELY!
WIGGLE
WIGGLE
うね
うね
HUM... UM... UM...
WIGGLE
WIGGLE
WIGGLE
WIGGLE
うね
うね
うね
うね

URGH!!!
VOILA! YOU SAW IT BEND, RIGHT?!
OU JUST USED YOUR HANDS!!

THIS IS WHAT YOU CALL A PSYCHIC POWER!
WITH STRICT TRAINING, YOU TOO, CAN HAVE THIS GIFT!
"TRAINING," SHE SAYS...
BOY, WHAT WOULD WE EVER DO WITHOUT YOU...
RUSTLE RUSTLE
OH, I HAVE ONE MORE THING...!
?!!
CHECK OUT THIS MYSTIFYING PHOTO OF A U.F.O.!!
THE STRING THAT IT'S HANGING FROM IS RIGHT THERE!!
THIS U.F.O. HAS BEEN WITNESSED ALL OVER THE WORLD!
THEY SAY IT APPEARS WHEN HISTORY IS ABOUT TO CHANGE!
BUT THIS NEXT ONE TOPS THEM ALL!

TUMBLE
ころん…!!
IT'S A MATERIA STONE!
THIS STONE IS A FRAGMENT OF A MYSTERIOUS CRYSTAL THAT COMES FROM THE MESOPOTAMIAN CIVILIZATION!
SNICKER
フフフ…!
THERE'S NONE LIKE IT IN THE WORLD TODAY!
IT JUST LOOKS LIKE A ROCK...!!
I'M ONLY SHOWING IT TO YOU GUYS 'CAUSE YOU'RE SPECIAL!
THIS ISN'T EVERYTHING FROM MY COLLECTION! I'VE GOT LOTS MORE!
BUT I'LL SHOW YOU THOSE NEXT TIME!
I'M SURE WE CAN ALL WAIT 'TIL THEN...
BUT IT'S REALLY SOME-THING, HUH?

ON TOP OF SHIRAISHI-SAN, THE SMARTEST STUDENT IN OUR YEAR...
WE HAVE MIYAMURA-KUN FROM THE STUDENT COUNCIL.
YAMADA IS, WELL, ONE OF "THOSE GUYS," I GUESS.
THOSE GUYS?!

BUT THE FACT THAT ALL THREE OF YOU HAVE AN INTEREST IN THE SUPERNATURAL IS JUST... WOW!
!

SMILE
にこっ
WE'RE ALL GONNA BE REAL BUSY FROM HERE ON OUT!!
OKAY! I'M GOING BACK TO THE CLASS-ROOM!
SLAM
...

WH-WHAT DO WE DO NOW?!
SHE'S JOINING THIS CLUB BECAUSE SHE'S ACTUALLY INTERESTED IN THE... CLUB!
AFTER SEEING ALL THAT CLUB SPIRIT,
IT'S GONNA BE A LITTLE HARD TO TELL HER WE'RE ONLY HERE TO USE THE ROOM!
HMM.
AND IT'S NOT LIKE WE CAN JUST TELL HER OUR SECRET, EITHER!
WELL, I'M PRETTY SURE SHE DOESN'T HAVE ANY IDEA THAT YAMADA-KUN HAS THE POWER TO SWITCH BODIES.
World History
世界史
...TRUE! FOR NOW, THE BEST THING FOR US TO DO IS ACT LIKE WE'RE INTERESTED IN THE SUPER-NATURAL.

UH... BUT, STILL...
HEY, YOU GUYS!
BANG
RATTLE
RATTLE
RATTLE
CAN YOU LEND ME A HAND?!
ACK! WHAT THE HELL ARE YOU BRINGING IN?!!

CLEANING SUPPLIES!
THIS ROOM IS FILTHY FROM NOT BEING USED IN SO LONG, Y'KNOW?
TALK ABOUT OVER-KILL!
AND WHAT'S ALL THIS JUNK? THERE'S LOTS OF USELESS THINGS JUST LYING AROUND!

HEY, YAMADA! TAKE THIS GARBAGE OUT!
WHAT?! WHY DO I HAVE TO?!
YOU'RE A CLUB MEMBER, AREN'T YOU? DON'T YOU WANT A CLEAN CLUBROOM?

...
DUDE, WE GOTTA USE THE ROOM.
DO WHAT ITOU SAYS, MAN...
DAMN IT...! THIS IS BECOMING A REAL PAIN!!

ドシャッ
WHUMP
PHEW...

THAT STUPID GIRL...!
PAT
ぱん
PAT
ぱん
MAKING ME DO ALL THE GRUNT WORK!

HAVING HER AROUND IS GONNA BE A PROBLEM...
AT THIS RATE, I WON'T BE ABLE TO SWITCH BODIES WITH SHIRAISHI WHENEVER I WANT TO...

DAMN...!
AND JUST WHEN WE GOT THE CLUBROOM, TOO!

UH!
WHAT THE?
ITOU'S NOT HERE?
ALONE
ポツ──ン

YEAH... SHE WAS CLEANING THE ROOM NOT TOO LONG AGO, THOUGH...
OH, REALLY...

WELL... WHAT DO YOU KNOW?!
NOW THAT I THINK ABOUT IT, ITOU WON'T BE AROUND ALL THE TIME!

WE'LL HAVE PLENTY OF TIME TO SWITCH BODIES, AFTER ALL!
B-BY THE WAY, SHIRAISHI...

YOU WANT ME TO TAKE A TEST FOR YOU IN YOUR ELECTIVE CLASS?
SURE, I DON'T MIND.
BAM
Y-YOU DON'T?!
NOPE.
BESIDES, IT'S BEEN A WHILE SINCE THE LAST TIME WE SWITCHED BODIES...!
...
R-RIGHT!!

OKAY, THEN...
MM-HMM.
THA-THUMP
THA-THUMP

SLIDE
HEY! YOU GUYS KNOW WHERE THE MOP-CLOTHS ARE?!
EEP!
JUMP
ER... UH...
?
YAMADA, YOU'RE ALREADY DONE TAKING THE GARBAGE OUT?!
UH... Y-YEAH!
THEN, GO LOOK FOR THE MOP-CLOTHS FOR ME, WILL YA!
HUH?! M-ME AGAIN?!
YOU SHOULD DO WHAT SHE SAYS.
...

OKAY, HERE...!!
GROAN
ずーん
!
NICE, SHE'S NOT HERE ANYMORE!
OKAY, SHIRAISHI! IT'S NOW OR NEVER!!
OKAY...

TREMBLE
プルプル
HEY, YAMADA! HOW'S THAT CLOTH SEARCH COMIN' ALONG?
ガラッ
SLIDE
ばっ
JUMP
GREAT! NOW FIND THE FLOOR WAX. THANKS!
NOT AGAIN?!!

SLIDE
AND IT KEPT GOING ON LIKE THIS...
NEXT, FILL A BUCKET FULL OF WATER!
ALWAYS MISSING THE CHANCE TO SWITCH WITH SHIRAISHI BY A HAIR...
CAN THIS GIRL GIMME A FRIGGIN' BREAK?!
AAAARRRGH!!!
ALL WHILE THE TEST WAS FAST APPROACHING!
DUDE, YOU STILL HAVEN'T SWITCHED BODIES?
MAYBE WE SHOULD JUST CALL IT A DAY.
NO WAY!!
MY GRADES ARE ON THE LINE HERE!!
JUST DO IT YOURSELF FOR ONCE.
HEY, YAMA-DA!
!!
OKAY! JUST LEAVE THIS TO ME!

HEY, ITOU-SAN!
THERE'S AN IMPORTANT JOB FOR YOU TOO, Y'KNOW?

WOULD YOU MIND TAKING THIS TO THE STUDENT COUNCIL OFFICE AND HANDING IT TO THE PRESIDENT?
?

MY CLUB NOTICE FORM?
RIGHT! I TOTALLY FORGOT!

I'LL BE RIGHT BACK!
SHUT
OH, NO YOU WON'T ...!

OUR PRESIDENT LOVES TO TALK, Y'SEE?
SO HE PROBABLY WON'T LET HER GO UNTIL THE BELL RINGS.
NICELY DONE, MAN!!

WE BETTER HURRY IF WE DON'T WANT TO MISS OUR AFTERNOON CLASSES!
R-RIGHT!
WE'RE IN A BIT OF A BIND...

WE CAN'T JUST LET ITOU-SAN DO HER OWN THING LIKE THIS...
THA-THUMP THA-THUMP
WITH THAT SAID, IT'S NOT LIKE THERE'S ANOTHER PLACE FOR US TO USE, EITHER...

HMM ...
URK!

A...
AHHHH!!!
OH MY GOD!!!
HUH?!
OH, NO...

WH-WHAT ARE YOU DOING HERE?!
WEREN'T YOU SUPPOSED TO GO SUBMIT YOUR CLUB NOTICE FORM?!
I DID... BUT THE PRESIDENT WASN'T THERE...!
WHAT?!
I THOUGHT IT WAS STRANGE...

To be continued in Volume 2

YOSHIKAWA'S ROOM

A PLACE WHERE YOSHIKAWA CAN EXPRESS HERSELF FREELY

To all my readers, both old and new,

Hello, my name is Yoshikawa!!

Thanks for picking up the first volume!
So, did you like the story?

It's pretty tough depicting the characters (for example, when the girl Urara's body is inhabited by the boy Yamada, she becomes **bowlegged**), and although I try to pay attention to the slight movements of the characters when I draw them, it's still really difficult!! But "switching bodies" is a fresh, new idea, so it's also true that I had a lot of fun illustrating the story. However, I feel like I still have a lot to learn in order to convey these characters better.

While preparing to drawing this story, all I did was have fun, doing thing like taking the staff on a trip overseas and playing games, so maybe I should've practiced drawing a bit more… But I have no regrets!! From now on, I'm going to do my very best!!

And so, this story is still just beginning, but things are going to get very interesting, so get excited for what's to come! Well, that's all from me this time!

Translation Notes

Grades/years in a Japanese High School, page 8

Japan's education system divides grades or years differently than the U.S. system. Both systems have 12 years of education before college, but in Japan, elementary school is for six years, junior high is for three years, and high school is for another three years. The key difference here is that Japanese high schools are not four years long. If the titular character, Yamada, were in his second year of high school in America, he would be in the 10th grade, making him 15-16 years old, but in Japan he is one year ahead, making him 16-17 years old. It should also be noted that his next year will be his last year in high school, which explains why his classmates are concerned about college in this story.

Westminster Quarters, page 25

The bell chime that is being expressed in this scene is a very specific melody that people who have lived in Japan or Taiwan are likely to be familiar with. This melody is commonly referred to as Westminster Quarters, in reference to the place where it is famously played, the clock tower at the Palace of Westminister in London, England. In Japan and Taiwan, this melody is used to signal the beginning or end of a school period. In this scene, the reader can understand that Yamada-kun (in Shiraishi's body) has to get to class.

Japanese bra sizes, page 127

In Japan, bra sizing is fairly different, and even the way that bras are made is not the same as it is in the United States. This is to accommodate the body shapes and features of the Japanese population, which are understandably different from many Western countries. One loose rule for figuring out the equivalent cup in the American sizing standard, is to just go down one letter, so in this case, Shiraishi's E-cup might be a D-cup in the United States.

School cleaning duties, page 189

Unlike in the United States, it is common for Japanese students to clean their own school. For the most part, Japanese schools do not employ janitors, and it is customary for students to form groups to clean classrooms, hallways, and courtyards during the designated cleaning time. Another interesting difference in regard to cleaning in Japan, is that instead of a regular mop, it is often the case that a cleaning cloth called a *zoukin* is used to dust and mop floors. If you watch anime or read manga that involves a Japanese shrine or temple, you may have seen this cloth being used to clean the wooden floors in a scene or two.

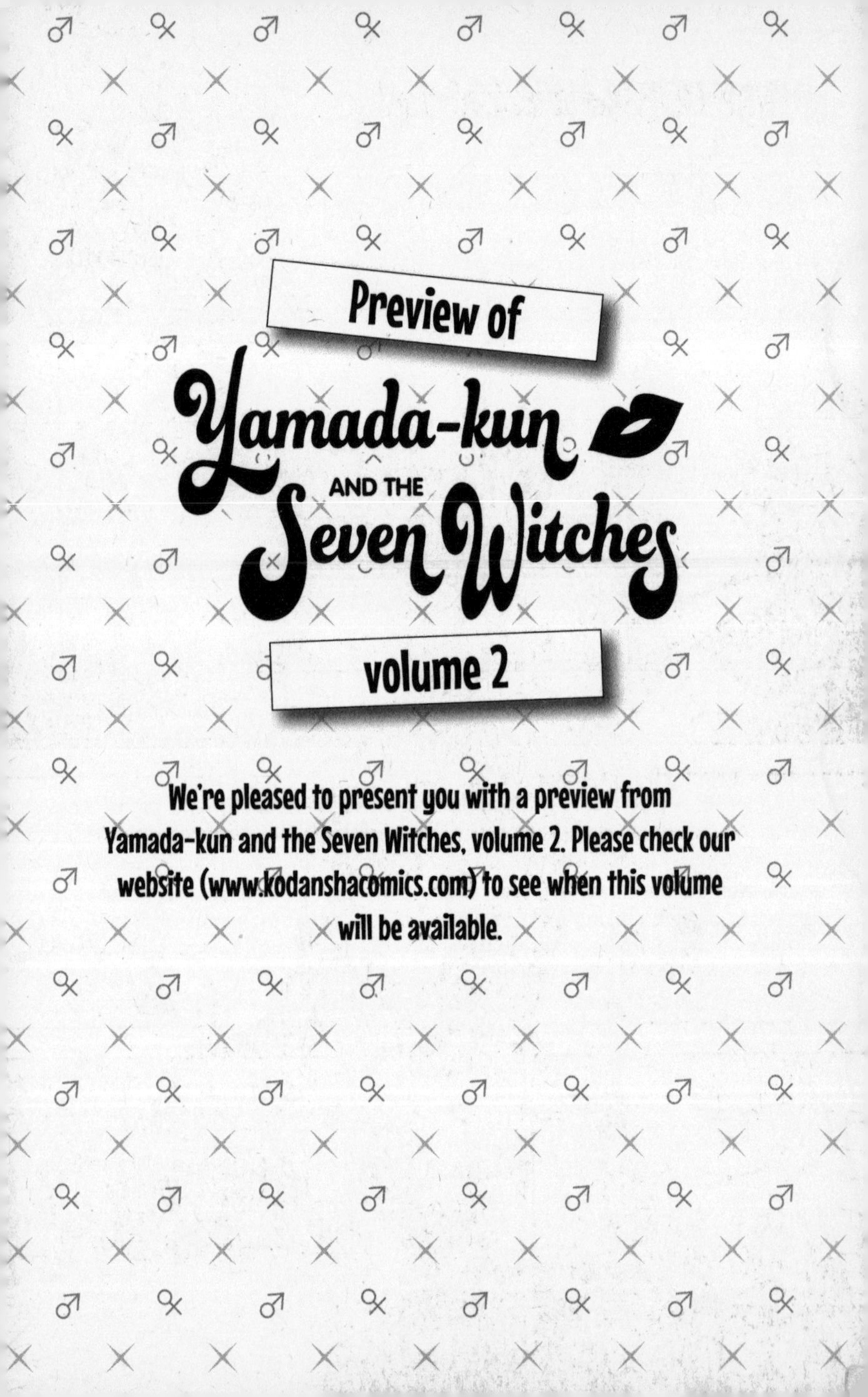
Preview of
Yamada-kun
AND THE
Seven Witches
volume 2
We're pleased to present you with a preview from Yamada-kun and the Seven Witches, volume 2. Please check our website (www.kodanshacomics.com) to see when this volume will be available.

CHAPTER 8: My Shiraishi-san...

BAM
2年B組の山田竜と白石うららはデキている!!
Ryu Yamada and Urara Shiraishi from Class 2-B are an item!!
山田
Yamada
白石
Shiraishi
College Entrance Seminar Applications
進学セミナー申込書類
MURMUR
MURMUR
MURMUR
!!?
WHA ?!
WHAT THE HELL IS THIS?!
山田
Yamada
白石
Shiraishi

DID YOU HEAR? YAMADA AND SHIRAISHI-SAN KISSED YESTERDAY!
NO WAY! REALLY?!
ARE THEY GOING OUT?
HUH?! WE'RE NOT!!
GET OUT OF THE WAY!!
山田竜と
白石うららは
デキている!!
EEK!
I SAID, LEMME THROUGH!!
WHOA!
DAMN! WHAT THE HELL, MAN?!
RIP
RIP
RIP
THIS ISN'T A JOKE!!
HEY! LOOK AT THIS!

IT SAYS YAMADA AND SHIRAISHI-SAN KISSED!
DAMN YOU, YAMADA!
IT CAN'T BE! MY SHIRAISHI-SAN...?
THERE'S EVEN A FLYER?!!
GIVE 'EM TO ME!
WH-WHAT THE?!
AARGH !!!
EEK!

DAMN IT! THIS IS GETTING OUT OF CONTROL!
CRUMPLE
WHO THE HELL IS BEHIND ALL THIS?!
APPEAR
OH? DON'T TELL ME YOU ALREADY FORGOT WHAT HAPPENED YESTERDAY!

I THOUGHT I WAS PRETTY CLEAR! YOU'RE NOT GETTING AWAY WITH THIS!!

FLAP
YOU'RE GONNA PAY!!
ITOU...! SO THIS IS ALL YOUR DOING!

JUST LETTING YOU KNOW... THIS IS FAR FROM OVER!
WHAT?!
CLICK
CLACK
YOU TRAMPLED ALL OVER MY FEELINGS FOR THIS CLUB...
AND I'M GONNA MAKE SURE YOU THOROUGHLY REGRET IT!

WHY, Y-YOU...!
HMPH! HOW TRIVIAL!

MIYAMURA!
LEAVE IT ALONE. WHAT'S THE POINT OF FIGHTING HER?
STILL... THAT RUMOR IS GONNA SPREAD THROUGH THE WHOLE SCHOOL!
DON'T LET IT GET TO YOU... PEOPLE END UP FORGETTING ABOUT RUMORS LIKE THIS, ANYWAY.
BESIDES, WE'RE NOT COMPLETELY BLAMELESS, EITHER!

TH- THAT'S TRUE, BUT...
BUT...

IF THESE THINGS KEEP HAPPENING...
2-B

COULD THE RUMORS BE TRUE?
SHE KISSED YAMADA?!

I KNEW IT...

SHE'S ALL ALONE AGAIN...

Yamada-kun and the Seven Witches volume 1 is a work of fiction. Names, characters, places, and incidents are the products of the author's imagination or are used fictitiously. Any resemblance to actual events, locales, or persons, living or dead, is entirely coincidental.

A Kodansha Comics Trade Paperback Original.

Published in the United States by Kodansha Comics,
an imprint of Kodansha USA Publishing, LLC, New York.

Publication rights for this English edition arranged through Kodansha Ltd., Tokyo.

First published in Japan in 2012 by Kodansha Ltd., Tokyo, as *Yamada-kun to Nananin no Majo* volume 1.

ISBN 978-1-63236-068-7

Printed in the United States of America.

www.kodanshacomics.com

9 8 7 6 5 4 3 2 1

Translator: David Rhie
Lettering: Sara Linsely
Editing: Ajani Oloye
Kodansha Comics Edition Cover Design: Phil Balsman